Human Resource Management in Early Internationalised SMEs

Small- and medium-sized enterprises (SMEs) are increasingly viewed as valuable contributors to the global economy, which translates into their importance in business literature and academic research. Recent studies suggest that there exists a substantial variety of international activities pursued by SMEs expanding abroad, with a prominent presence of early internationalised enterprises, including born global. Despite the acknowledgement of the importance of human capital for SME internationalisation, there is a persistent knowledge gap concerning HR practices in this context. Until now, researchers investigating the accelerated internationalisation of SMEs have focused either on the human capital of decision-makers or selected attributes of employees, although these have only been at the pre-entry or entry stages. Thus, activities performed after entering foreign markets remain. This book attempts to reduce this gap and contribute to the body of knowledge concerning HR practices in early internationalised SMEs with an emphasis on the post-entry phase.

By taking such an approach, this volume integrates two streams of research: HRM in the SMEs and international business. It provides managers of SMEs with useful information on dealing with internationalisation-related challenges by means of various practices including work structuring, recruitment and selection, training and development, employee appraisal and remuneration, and performance management. The discussion of these issues is based upon data from a survey conducted in 200 SMEs and case studies exemplifying HR practices in early internationalised small and medium enterprises. It offers academic researchers, postgraduate students, and reflective practitioners a state-of-the-art overview of managing human resources in small and medium enterprises expanding internationally, including both accelerated and incremental paths.

Joanna Purgał-Popiela is a Professor in the Department of Human Capital Management at Cracow University of Economics, Poland.

Urban Pauli is a Professor in the Department of Human Capital Management at Cracow University of Economics, Poland.

Aleksy Pocztowski is a Professor and Chair in the Department of Human Capital Management at Cracow University of Economics, Poland.

Routledge Focus on Business and Management

The fields of business and management have grown exponentially as areas of research and education. This growth presents challenges for readers trying to keep up with the latest important insights. *Routledge Focus on Business and Management* presents small books on big topics and how they intersect with the world of business research.

Individually, each title in the series provides coverage of a key academic topic, while collectively, the series forms a comprehensive collection across the business disciplines.

Neuroscience and Entrepreneurship Research
Researching Brain-Driven Entrepreneurship
Víctor Pérez Centeno

Proposal Writing for Business Research Projects
Peter Samuels

Systems Thinking and Sustainable Healthcare Delivery
Ben Fong

Gender Diversity and Inclusion at Work
Divergent Views from Turkey
Zeynep Özsoy, Mustafa Şenyücel and Beyza Oba

Management and Visualisation
Seeing Beyond the Strategic
Gordon Fletcher

For more information about this series, please visit: www.routledge.com/ Routledge-Focus-on-Business-and-Management/book-series/FBM

Human Resource Management in Early Internationalised SMEs

Joanna Purgał-Popiela,
Urban Pauli, and
Aleksy Pocztowski

Routledge
Taylor & Francis Group

NEW YORK AND LONDON

First published 2023
by Routledge
605 Third Avenue, New York, NY 10158

and by Routledge
4 Park Square, Milton Park, Abingdon, Oxon, OX14 4RN

*Routledge is an imprint of the Taylor & Francis Group, an
informa business*

This book has been financed by the subsidy granted to Cracow
University of Economics for maintaining research potential

ISBN: 978-1-032-33518-6 (hbk)
ISBN: 978-1-032-33519-3 (pbk)
ISBN: 978-1-003-31997-9 (ebk)

DOI: 10.4324/9781003319979

Typeset in Times New Roman
by MPS Limited, Dehradun

Contents

    *4.1   Theoretical background and conceptual
           framework 64*
    *4.2   Research instruments in quantitative and
           qualitative studies 71*
    *4.3   Presentation of research procedure and
           samples 74*

**5   HRM practices in the investigated
    companies – empirical findings**   80

    5.1   Research context 80
    5.2   Analysis of quantitative results 85
    5.3   Presentation of case studies 91
    5.4   Cross-case analysis 103

6   Conclusions   110

    References   118
    Index   136

Figures

Tables

1 Introduction

Small- and medium-sized enterprises (SMEs) are increasingly viewed as valuable contributors to the global economy, which translates into their importance in business literature and academic research (Krishnan & Scullion, 2017, p. 431). Recent studies suggest that there exists a substantial variety of international strategies and activities pursued by SMEs expanding abroad (Kuivalainen et al., 2012; Deligianni et al., 2015; Dominguez & Mayrhofer, 2017), with a prominent presence of early internationalised enterprises, including born global firms (Rialp et al., 2005; Romanello & Chiarvesio, 2019). The specificity of SMEs has been recognised in HRM literature (Sheehan, 2014) and is considered to be a severe constraint on the adoption of HRM practices that have been effectively employed by large organisations (Festing et al., 2013; Harney & Alkhalaf, 2020). This problem also affects SMEs operating internationally.

Interestingly, despite the acknowledgement of the importance of human capital for SME internationalisation (Paul et al., 2017; Buzavaite & Korsakiene, 2019; Chandra et al., 2020), there is a persistent knowledge gap concerning HRM practices in this context (Francioni et al., 2016, p. 207; Paul et al., 2017, p. 334). Moreover, of the sparse empirical works addressing these issues, almost none concern the early and rapid internationalisation of SMEs (notable exceptions include Isidor et al., 2011; Glaister et al., 2014; Ripollé et al., 2018; Breuillot, 2021). Until now, researchers investigating the accelerated internationalisation of SMEs have focused either on the human capital of decision-makers or selected attributes of employees, although these have only been at the pre-entry or entry stages (Onkelinx et al., 2016). Thus, activities performed after entering foreign markets remain understudied (Knight & Liesch, 2016; Ciszewska-Mlinarič et al., 2020); with this book, we attempt to reduce this gap.

DOI: 10.4324/9781003319979-1

The overall objective of this book is to outline the role of HRM in the specific context of SMEs that initiated operations in foreign markets shortly after their inception. The scope of HRM here includes HRM strategy and professionalisation; HRM practices and bundles (configurations) of these practices; and outcomes resulting from these practices. The focus on the aforementioned context arises from specific challenges related to the small size of the firm, namely the limited applicability of HRM practices developed in large multinationals and the accelerated internationalisation. Regarding the latter, it should be emphasised that early internationalised firms (EIFs), including born globals, learn differently to SMEs internationalising incrementally (Schwens & Kabst, 2009; Ciszewska-Mlinarič et al., 2020). Moreover, after the rapid course of the initial stages in their expansion, in which key drives are the entrepreneurs' characteristics and background, EIFs face entirely different problems of the post-entry phase (Gabrielsson et al., 2014; Rastrollo-Horrillo & Martin-Armario, 2019; Romanello & Chiarvesio, 2019). More specifically, to survive and grow in the long term, they need an adequate base of knowledge embedded in human and relational resource as well as the organisational capabilities to acquire, develop, deploy, and mobilise these resources (Romanello & Chiarvesio, 2017; Breuillot, 2021). However, there is dearth of empirical studies focussing on these issues.

This book reduces the gap in the extant knowledge on HRM in the post-entry stage by addressing the research problem concerning the role that HRM plays in early internationalised SMEs after their entry to foreign markets. Consequently, our theoretical considerations and empirical study are aimed at determining the following: how important HRM is in these companies regarding the specific challenges they face; what configurations of HRM practices are used by EIFs in respect of their different trajectories of post-entry internationalisation; how these practices contribute to company performance; in what way HRM practices adopted in these entities resemble the approaches followed by late internationalisers. In our search for answers to the aforementioned questions, we adopted a mixed research design that relies on analyses of quantitative and qualitative data collected from the survey and in-depth interviews.

The quantitative data stem from a sample of 200 randomly selected Polish-based SMEs that perform export activities and achieved at least the level of 25% FSTS (foreign sales to total sales ratio). The qualitative data consist of transcribed in-depth interviews with decision-makers in eight purposively selected early internationalised SMEs. Responding to calls for unified criteria in research on early/rapidly internationalised firms (Romanello & Chiarvesio, 2019), and in line with the prevalent operationalisation of these companies (Kuivalainen et al., 2012; Knight & Liesch, 2016; Øyna, & Alon, 2018), we adopted the operational definition by Knight and Cavusgil (2004) that introduces the maximum threshold of a three-year period from inception to the beginning of international operation combined with the required share of foreign sales, i.e. at least 25% of total sales.

The remaining content of the book that follows this introduction consists of four chapters and conclusions.

Chapter 2 outlines the specifics of the early and rapid internationalisation of SMEs. It begins with a discussion on the role of SMEs in the world economy, with an emphasis on current trends and forms of activity in the global and European market. It then focuses on the internationalisation of SMEs, including the internal and external determinants of this process. The last part of the chapter presents a comprehensive and nuanced portrait of early internationalised SMEs which emphasises the internal heterogeneity of these enterprises and highlights the features that distinguish them from other participants in the global market.

Chapter 3 aims at recognising the implications of early internationalisation for managing human resources in SMEs. Thus, our discussion begins with the HRM specificity in SMEs with the emphasis on the prominent role played by owners/top managers in the above domain of activity. We then analyse the opportunities and limits of the transferability of HRM practices from large multinationals to the context of international SMEs. Finally, we focus on the process of accelerated internationalisation to recognise HR-related problems occurring in the consecutive phases of this process and define the state of empirical-based knowledge concerning these issues.

Chapter 4 provides detailed information on the methodological aspects of our empirical study. In the first part, we discuss the theoretical foundations and develop a conceptual framework underlying the analysis of data. We then outline the research design which includes, inter alias, the operationalisation of key constructs, the development of research tools, the sampling strategy, and data collection methods. Finally, we describe the empirical material, including details of the participants of the research and the companies they represent.

Chapter 5 presents the empirical findings of our quantitative and qualitative studies. It begins with a discussion of research context, more specifically, the CEE region and Poland as a source of institutional pressures on the international activities and personnel function of SMEs. The quantitative data are then analysed, including the overview and comparing of contextual factors characterising early and late internationalised SMEs as well as HRM practices adopted in both groups and their outcomes. In this section, we also discuss the differences in configurations of HRM practices used in various categories of EIFs. The two consecutive parts of this chapter are devoted to selected cases of early internationalised SMEs. Initially, each case is considered separately, then, following the conceptual framework, we conduct a cross-sectional analysis to identify and explain the differences and similarities between the cases.

The last part of the book constitutes a synthesis of the empirical results. Based on these findings, we respond to the research questions posed in the methodological chapter. We also discuss the limitations of our study and formulate implications for further research and practice.

With this book, we seek to enrich the extant knowledge concerning HRM practices in early internationalised SMEs with an emphasis on the post-entry phase. By taking such an approach, we make an attempt to integrate two streams of research, namely HRM in the SMEs and international business. Having acknowledged the practical relevance of the considered issues, we also provide original empirical findings that demonstrate how the aforementioned companies deal with internationalisation-related challenges by means of various practices including work structuring, recruitment and selection, training and development, employee appraisal and remuneration, and performance management. Finally, we hope that this book offers academic researchers, postgraduate students, and reflective practitioners a state-of-the-art overview of managing human resources in SMEs expanding internationally, including both accelerated and incremental paths.

2 The context and nature of early internationalised SMEs

2.1 Small and medium enterprises as participants of the global economy

Small and medium enterprises play an important role in the economies of all countries. According to OECD data, regardless of the level of a country's development, at least around 60–70% of all workers are employed by SMEs employ (OECD, n.d. a). In more developed countries, this share is even higher. Additionally, micro, small, and medium enterprises (MSMEs) account for over 95% of all enterprises (WTO, 2016). In total, micro firms account for 82.9%, small firms for 13.8%, and medium enterprises for 3.3%. In the case of developed countries, the share of micro firms is higher (87.1%) than in developing countries (80.5%) (WTO, 2016). In Europe, the population of SMEs amounts to more than 25 million entities, these enterprises employ around 100 million people and account for more than one-half of Europe's GDP. This is why in European Commission documents, small and medium enterprises are perceived to be the backbone of the EU economy (European Commission, 2020). Similarly, the Office of the United States Trade Representatives claims that SMEs are the backbone of the US economy as 28 million American SMEs have accounted for nearly two-thirds of net new private sector jobs in recent decades (Office of the United States Trade Representatives, n.d.).

Additionally, SMEs are acknowledged to be the driver for the economy's development. These enterprises create innovative solutions, enhance resource efficiency, create networks, and increase social cohesion. By their economic activity, they spread new business solutions and knowledge between countries and regions, which can result in providing higher resilience to shocks.

Nevertheless, economic statistics indicate that small and medium enterprises are under-represented in international trade and they

DOI: 10.4324/9781003319979-2

account for a relatively small proportion of exports relative to their share of overall activity and employment (OECD, n.d. a). When analysing the level of engagement of SMEs in international trade, various types of activities are taken into account. The most common is the calculation of the share and value of SMEs in direct import and export both with regard to the number of enterprises and the value of trade. However, the non-equity contractual agreements, foreign direct investments, other forms of equity agreements and indirect export (which refers to supplying goods and services to domestic firms that export) are also included when analysing the international trade activity of SMEs (WTO, 2016).

Taking into account the number of enterprises engaged in international trade, in many countries, it is MSMEs that account for the highest share. However, the overall value of these transactions is higher in the case of large enterprises rather than MSMEs. According to WTO calculations based on World Bank Enterprise Surveys covering over 25,000 SMEs (WTO, 2016), considering only direct participation in trade, micro firms and SMEs from developed countries represent the vast majority of trading firms – over 90% in many countries. On average, firms with fewer than 250 employees account for 78% of exporters in developed countries but only 34% of exports. SMEs are very active in building international cooperation but agreements very often cover a relatively low value of traded goods or services.

Similar findings, about the share of SMEs in international trade, were calculated with regard to EU SMEs. In 2019, in total intra-EU and extra-EU trade, 99% of importing companies and 98% of exporting companies were MSMEs. These values remained almost unchanged between 2015 and 2019 (Eurostat, 2021). However, when analysing the value of trade, the share of MSMEs is smaller than in the case of the number of enterprises. In 2019, MSMEs were assigned to 46% of EU imports of goods and 37% of EU exports of goods. The share of small entities in imports was at the level of 14% and in export 10%. For medium enterprises, these values were 21% and 20%, respectively (Eurostat, 2021).

2.1.1 Share of SMEs in international trade

On the basis of OECD data, it can be shown that the level and share of SME participation in international trade varies between countries. As far as import is concerned (Figure 2.1), the lowest share of SMEs that participate in international trade is assigned to the Netherlands where the share of small enterprises is at the level of 10%. Additionally,

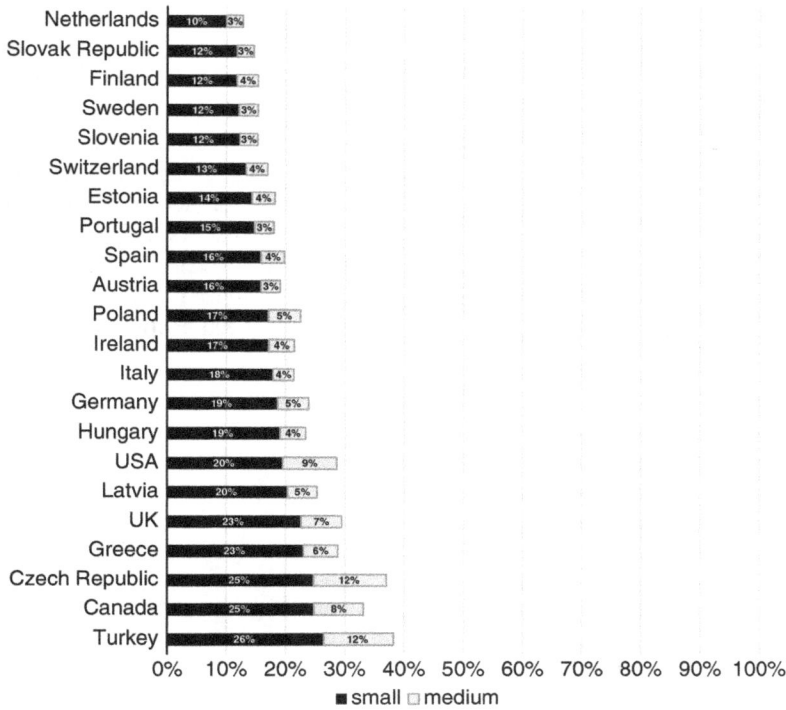

Figure 2.1 Share of small and medium enterprises in the total number of importing companies in selected OECD countries.

Source: OECD, 2022.

Note: For the UK and the USA, the data refer to 2018; the remaining countries relate to 2019.

in four countries – Finland, Slovak Republic, Slovenia, and Sweden – small importers accounted for 12%. By contrast, in countries like Turkey, Canada, and Czech Republic, one out of every four importing enterprises is small. Thus, it can be concluded that the share of small enterprises in all importing companies is very diverse.

The difference between the share of medium enterprises in all importers is not as big as in the case of small entities, ranging from 9% to 12%. The smallest share of small importers relates to Austria, the Netherlands, Portugal, Slovak Republic, Slovenia, and Sweden. The highest share (12%) relates to the Czech Republic and Turkey.

In general, on the basis of the presented data, it can be concluded that the share of SMEs in importing companies is very diversified and ranges from only 13% in the case of the Netherlands and up to 48% in the case of Turkey.

Analyses of the share of SMEs in exporting companies (Figure 2.2) show that SME involvement in this kind of international trade flow is higher than in the case of import, ranging from 18% to 51%. In the case of small companies, the lowest share (14%) is assigned to the Netherlands and Slovenia. The highest share is assigned to the Czech Republic (31%) and Greece (30%). Thus, the dispersion of the involvement of small enterprises in export is at the level of 17%.

In the case of medium enterprises, the lowest share (4%) is assigned to Slovenia, with the highest assigned to the Czech Republic (20%).

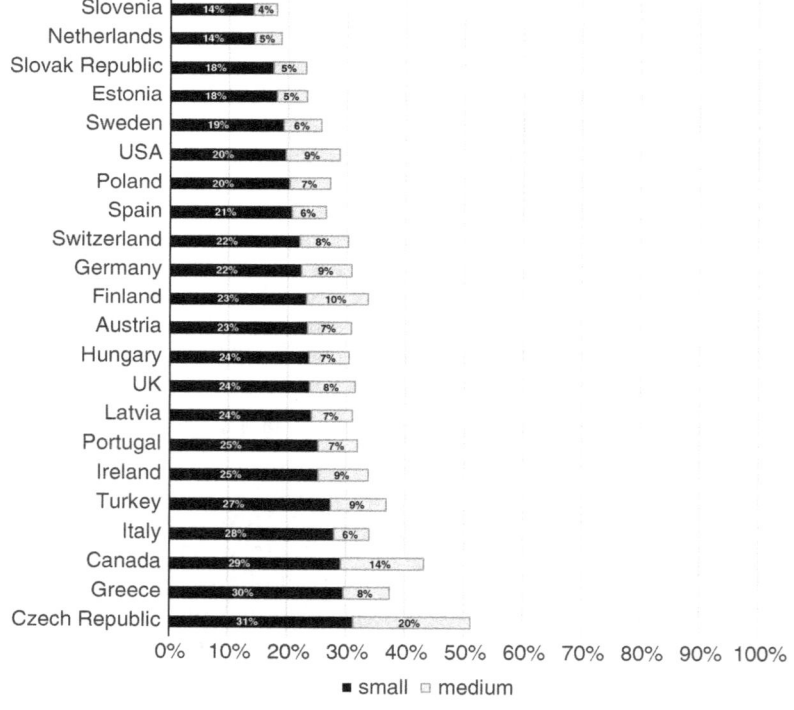

Figure 2.2 Share of small and medium enterprises in the total number of exporting companies in selected OECD countries.

Source: OECD, 2022.

Note: For the UK and the USA, the data refer to 2018; the remaining countries relate to 2019.

In the case of export, the dispersion level between the share of the involvement of small and medium enterprises is similar. Nevertheless, it should be added that in general, the share of SME involvement in export activities is higher than in import.

2.1.2 Share of SMEs in total international trade value

Taking into account the value of SME import in the total import value (Figure 2.3), it can be observed that the differences between particular countries are significant. The share of American SMEs in the total import value is at the level of 15% while in Estonia, it is calculated to be four times higher.

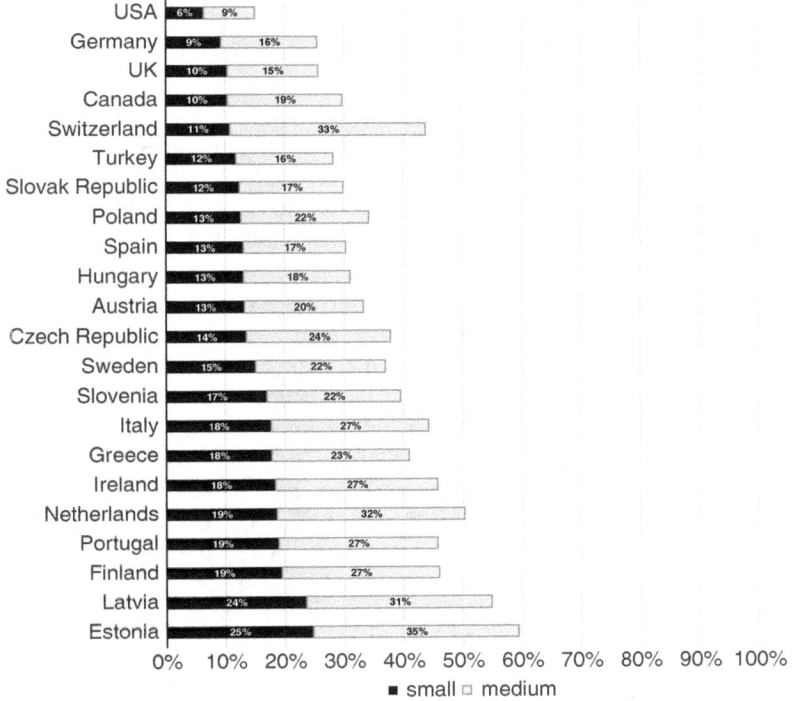

Figure 2.3 Share of SME's import value in total import value in selected OECD countries.

Source: OECD, 2022.

Note: For the UK and the USA, the data refer to 2018; the remaining countries relate to 2019.

When analysing only small companies, the lowest share (6%) in import value relates to the USA. This share is also relatively low in Germany and is valued at 9%. By contrast, in such countries as Latvia and Estonia, the share of small entities in trade value is at the level of 25% one-fourth.

With regard to medium enterprises, American companies, with their 9% share in import value, seem to be outliers, as it is the only country with a share below 10%. In most countries, the share of this type of organisation is around 20% while in countries like Estonia, Latvia, the Netherlands, and Switzerland, it is about one-third.

In the case of share in import value, some significant differences can be observed as in the case of small enterprises, in which these shares vary from 6% to 25%, and for medium companies, for which the range is 9% to 35%.

When analysing export-related data (Figure 2.4), it can be observed that in general, the share of SMEs in the export value is similar to the share in the import value.

The lowest share in the export value relates to Irish and American small enterprises (4% and 5%, respectively). On the contrary, nearly 20% of the export value is generated by small firms in Turkey, Estonia, and Latvia.

American and German medium enterprises contribute the least to their national export values with shares at the level of 10% and 13%. The highest share of export value relates to Estonian medium enterprises (42%) and to companies from the Netherlands (37%).

It should be acknowledged that in the case of export there are the largest differences. The share of small enterprises varies from 4% to 22%, and in the case of medium companies, the share varies from 10% to 42%.

On the basis of the presented data, it can be concluded that SMEs in analysed countries are relatively more active in export than in import. Moreover, on the basis of the analysis of the internationalisation of SMEs (European Commission, 2010), there is a negative correlation between the size of the SME's home country population and its level of international activity. Countries such as Estonia, Denmark, Sweden, the Czech Republic and Slovenia have a much higher percentage of exporters than the EU average of 25%. Germany, France and the UK score below average.

When analysing data referring to the size and value of international trade, it can be observed that in general, the share of small enterprises in international trading entities is higher than their share in the value of international trade (Figure 2.5). In the case of import, in more than half of the investigated countries, the share of small entities in the number of all internationally active companies is higher than the share of small firms in the total import value. When the export is analysed, such a situation does not concern only Estonia and the Netherlands. In the case of medium enterprises, the situation is reversed. The share of international trade value

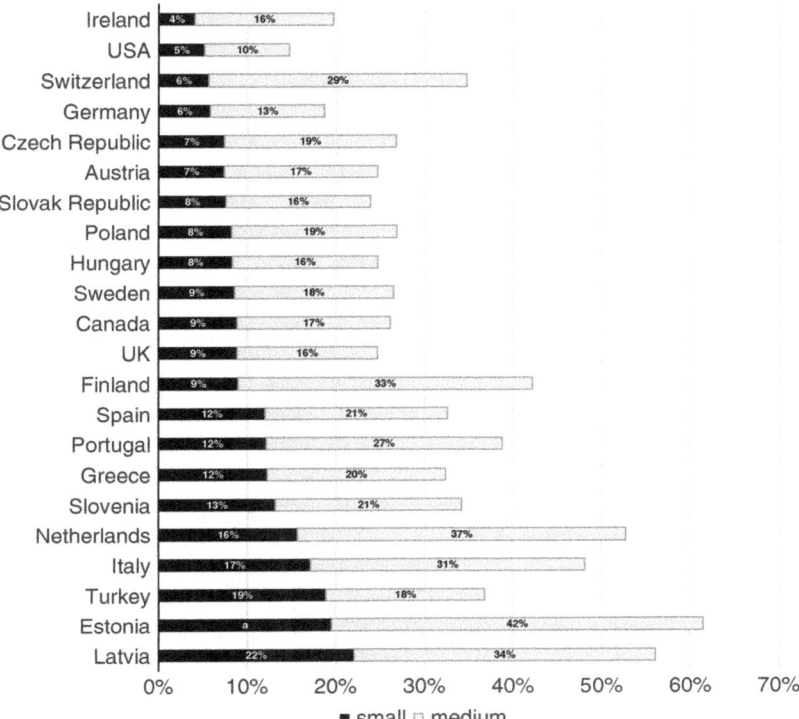

Figure 2.4 Share of SMEs export value in total export value in selected countries.

Source: OECD, 2022.

Note: For UK and the USA, the data refers to 2018; the remaining countries relate to 2019.

is higher than the share of medium enterprises in the total number of enterprises. Such a situation does not occur only in the USA (import) and the Czech Republic (Export).

2.1.3 The value of the international transactions of SMEs

The differences between small and medium enterprises in the share of international trade value mostly depend on the level of financial transfers generated by these companies. As presented in Figure 2.6, the average yearly value of transactions per company in a medium enterprise is much higher than in a small enterprise. Small enterprises' import transactions vary from 0.63 (Portugal) to 3.20 million USD

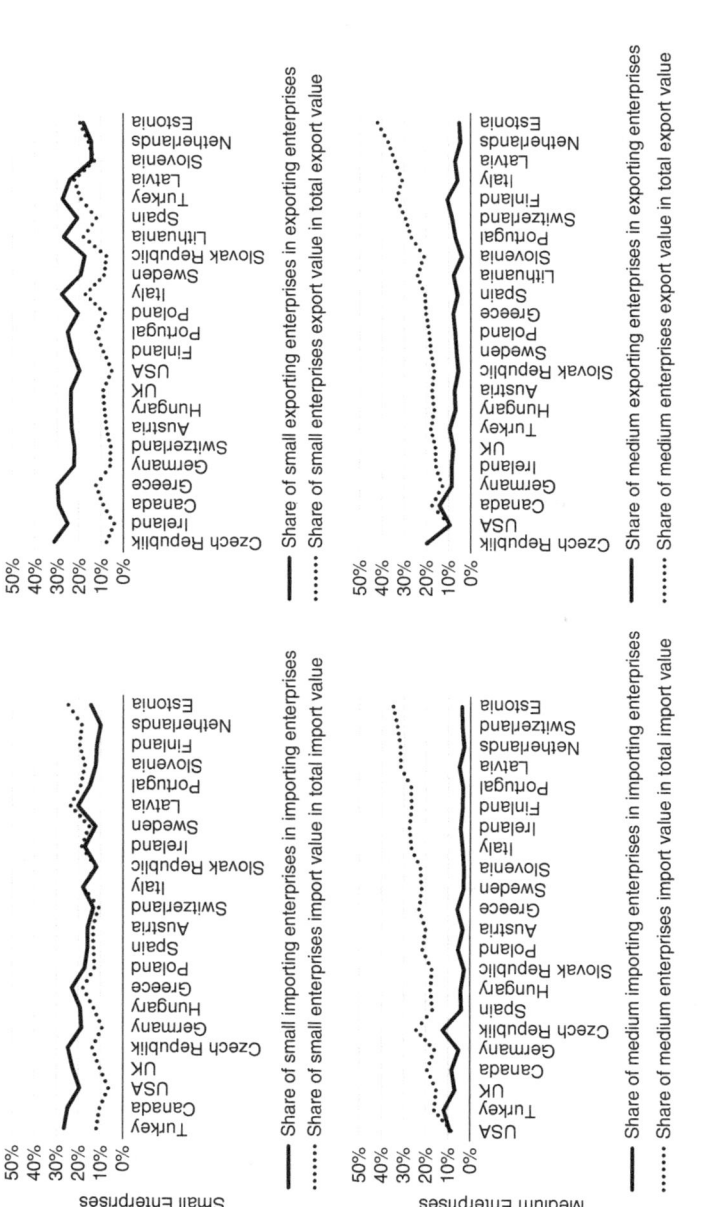

Figure 2.5 Comparison of the share of small and medium enterprises in international trading companies with their share in international trade value.

Source: OECD, 2022.

Note: For the UK and the USA, the data refer to 2018; the remaining countries relate to 2019.

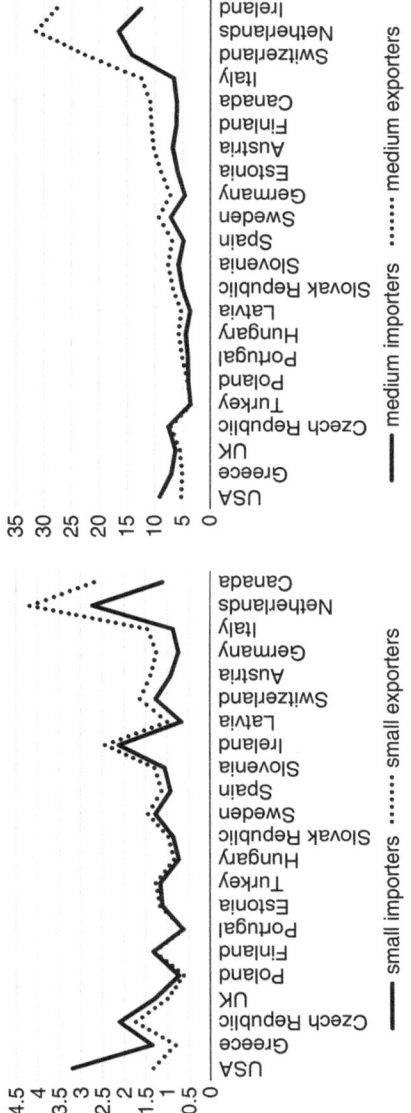

Figure 2.6 Average yearly import and export value per company (in millions USD).

Source: OECD, 2022.

Note: For UK and the USA, data are for 2018, for the remaining countries, data relates to 2019.

(USA) while in medium enterprises the range is from 3.55 (Turkey) to 16.55 (the Netherlands). The export transactions of small enterprises vary from 0.62 (Poland) to 4.19 million USD (The Netherlands) while in medium enterprises, the range is from 3.45 (Turkey) to 31.42 (The Netherlands). In general, regardless of the firm's size and with regard to both trade flows SMEs from the Netherlands generate the highest value of transactions per company yearly.

It is also worth noting that in most cases, the value of transactions generated by exporters is higher than that generated by importers. This situation does not apply to Poland, Finland, and Portugal in the case of small enterprises; and the Czech Republic, Greece, the UK, and the USA in the case of both small and medium organisations.

However, it should also be acknowledged that in almost all countries, except for the USA and Turkey, there are more importing than exporting companies whether they be small or medium (Figure 2.7). In the case of small enterprises, the highest ratio is calculated for Ireland (3.07), Canada (3.05), and Austria (2.81) which means that for every exporting company, there are nearly three that import. When analysing medium enterprises, the ratios are 2.26, 2.14, and 1.82 for these three countries, respectively, which means that for every exporting company, there are nearly two that import.

Based on the presented data, it can be confirmed that SMEs play a very important and active role in international trade. However, such a conclusion mostly reflects the situation in developed countries. According to WTO, among developing regions, Africa has the lowest export share at 3%, compared to 8.7% for developing Asia. Participation by SMEs in direct exports of services in developing

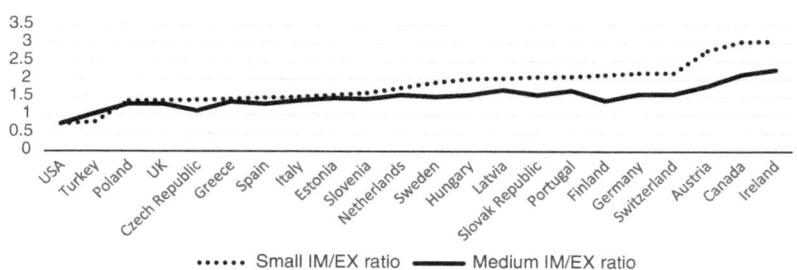

Figure 2.7 The ratio between the number of importing and exporting companies in selected OECD countries.

Source: OECD, 2022.

Note: For the UK and the USA data refer to 2018, for the remaining countries, data relates to 2019.

countries is very low, representing only 0.9% of total services sales compared to 31.9% for large enterprises (WTO, 2016).

2.1.4 Enhancing the participation of SMEs in international trade

Being part of international trade can be very fruitful for SMEs. According to EC analyses (European Commission, 2010), the benefits of cooperation with companies from other countries may relate to turnover, employment and innovation. When turnover is taken into account, more than 50% of SMEs that invest abroad and SMEs that are involved in international subcontracting, reported an increase in turnover, whereas for all SMEs, this was about 35%. Employment growth for exporting companies was calculated at the level of 7% (non-exporters 3%), for importing companies this value was at the level of 8% (non-importers 2%), for importing and exporting companies, it was at the level of 10% (others 3%) and for SMEs with FDI, it was at the level of 16% (others 4%). Additionally, 26% of internationally active SMEs introduced products or services that were new for their sector in their country (others 8%), and 11% of these SMEs introduced process innovations that were new for their sector in their country (others 3%).

Regardless of the type of international activities, SMEs often face some difficulties and obstacles when trying to enter foreign markets. Analyses of the international activity of SMEs made it possible to identify nearly fifty types of barriers that small and medium enterprises may encounter. These include both internal barriers (which refer to organisational resources and approaches to export business), and external barriers (related to the environments of the home and host countries). Among internal barriers, five categories were identified connected with informational barriers, human resource barriers, financial barriers, product and price barriers, and with distribution, logistics and promotion. In the group of external barriers, the following five categories were identified: procedural barriers, governmental barriers, customer and foreign competitor barriers, business environment barriers, tariff, and non-tariff barriers (OECD, n.d. b).

In order to help SMEs to internationalise and overcome existing or potential barriers, organisations at the national or regional level introduce SME supporting programmes. These programmes are mostly aimed at fostering export among SMEs. This is due to both the ratio of importing and exporting companies and to the average value of transactions per entity. As presented above, the average yearly export transactions per company are higher than in the case of import, but in general, there are more SME importers than exporters, which may negatively impact the trade balance. As an example, the European Union's programmes fostering cooperation with Asian or North American countries can be presented. Another example is initiatives undertaken by ASEAN, which are aimed not only at fostering cooperation between South-East Asian SMEs but also with European countries. There are also initiatives undertaken to reinforce transpacific economic cooperation. Despite the fact that direct activities are introduced by countries or organisations, it should be acknowledged that changes in the global economy as well as the level of ICT technology development support the internationalisation of SMEs. The facilitated flow of goods and services may cause these type of enterprises to become important actors in the global value chain. This is strengthened by the development of ICT, which causes the geographical distance to be no longer portrayed as an obstacle. There are many firms which may provide their services, sell goods or create cooperation with the use of the Internet.

All the circumstances discussed above cause the number of SMEs that are part of international trade to rise. As presented in Figure 2.8, the number of internationally active companies in the European Union has consequently been rising since 2014, but in the case of imports, an increase is steeper. Additionally, the number of enterprises in all three categories (small, medium, and large) has been similarly increasing. In the case of export, the number of large companies engaged in international trade rises more than in the case of medium and small enterprises.

In the case of Canada (Figure 2.9), similar to the EU countries, the rise in the number of importing companies is higher than the rise in the number of exporting companies. Additionally, it should be stated that there was a decrease in the number of exporting large companies between 2015 and 2018.

In the USA (Figure 2.10), the number of importing companies has been increasing consistently since 2014. The percentage change in subsequent years was similar for all three groups of companies (small, medium and large). In the case of export, there was an increase in the number of exporting companies only when taking into account large companies. Between 2014 and 2017, the number of exporting small and medium enterprises was decreasing. In the last year of the analyses, the number of exporting medium enterprises continued to decrease while the number of small exporters slightly increased.

The presented and discussed data confirm that SMEs are important participants of the global economy. They not only operate on country markets but also act internationally. They are involved in both importing and exporting activities as well as in other forms of agreements and direct

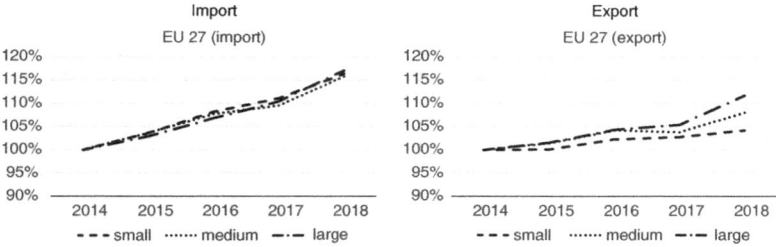

Figure 2.8 Trends in the number of internationally active SMEs in the EU between 2014 and 2018.

Source: OECD, 2022.

Note: The number of internationally active companies in 2014 was 100%.

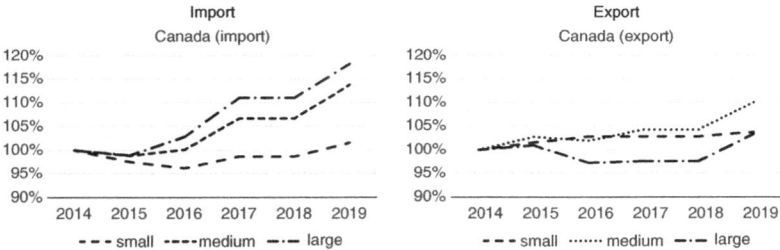

Figure 2.9 Trends in the number of internationally active SMEs in Canada between 2014 and 2018.

Source: OECD, 2022.

Note: The number of internationally active companies in 2014 was 100%.

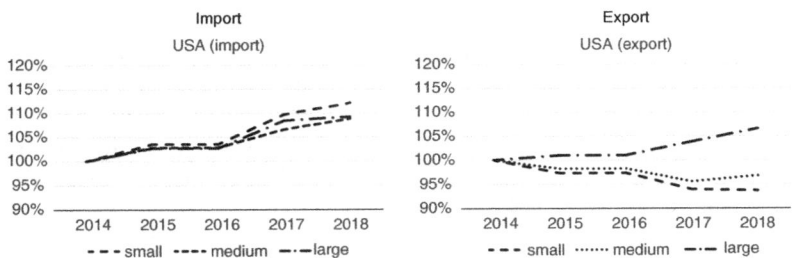

Figure 2.10 Trends in the number of internationally active SMEs in the USA between 2014 and 2018.

Source: OECD, 2022.

Note: The number of internationally active companies was 2014 is 100%.

investments. Additionally, they are involved in indirect export by supporting other exporting companies. Despite the fact that SMEs face many barriers in internationalisation, supporting programmes as well as changes in business environment cause the number of SMEs engaged in international activities to be rising. However, it should be acknowledged that there are many differences in the engagement of SMEs in international trade, and the level of the involvement varies significantly between countries. This situation stems mostly from the context these companies operate in.

2.2 Contextual factors determining SMEs activities

The importance of context-related issues in scientific research has gained more attention over the last two decades. Despite the fact that the analyses of the impact of particular factors on the performance of organisations were published even earlier, rapid changes in the business environment and the crises that firms had to face, have made it necessary to apply wider and deeper insight into circumstances that may impact on the functioning of firms.

In most cases, the environment in which companies have to operate is perceived as a threat due to its unpredictability and potentially negative impact on performance. This is why acronyms like VUCA (volatility, uncertainty, complexity, and ambiguity) or RUDE (rapidly changing, uncertain, dynamic, engaging) are used to characterise the context in scientific publications. However, it should also be stated that in some cases, these features of the environment may be a source of opportunities and may help to boost performance or act as a leverage in building a competitive position. The main conclusions that may be drawn on the basis of scientific literature state that contextual factors have a direct impact on organisations (be it positive or negative), and that research on any type of organisation should be embedded in a particular context.

In scientific publications, it is claimed that context may have a higher impact on SMEs rather than on large companies due to the scope and amount of resources that SMEs possess and due to their limited potential to shape the business environment. Such a situation refers to the so-called 'liability of smallness' which is manifested in a lack of resources and limited market information (Boocock & Anderson, 2003). However, features of SMEs such as flexibility and simplified decision-making processes (most decisions are made by the owner) can help in coping with changes that occur in dynamically changing circumstances.

The most frequently applied approach in defining context includes its internal and external dimensions. The external context covers issues related to social, political, economic, legal, technological, ecological and cultural factors. With regard to internal context, such factors as strategy business model, the technology used, the scope of resources, internal processes, managers/owners attitudes and competences, age and growth stages are taken into account (Jackson & Schuler, 1995). However, the context can be also analysed with regard to the three levels of organisation, market/industry/business sector and country. The organisational context refers to all the factors that are specific for a particular enterprise and includes all the components mentioned above as 'internal'. The market/ business sector context covers factors related with the market maturity, the number of competitors, supply chains, the number of potential customers and networks. Factors that can be analysed with regard to the national level include those mentioned above as external dimensions.

Taking into account the number of factors determining the context and the way they interlace, every particular organisation operates in the environment which is shaped by the variety of elements. Such a situation can be called 'polycontextuality' and refers to the existence of different facets of context (Child et al., 2022).

2.2.1 General classification of contextual factors

The variety of factors that create the context of the functioning of SMEs can be presented with the use of three levels – macro, meso, and micro.

The macro-level refers to all external factors that are specific for the country and impact all the enterprises regardless of their origin and size. At this level, the following dimensions are included social, political, economic, legal, technological, ecological, and cultural. All of these create specific circumstances which may support or limit the business activity of SMEs in the home country and also a willingness to inter-nationalise. For example, economic conditions may make it profitable for some companies to sell their goods abroad due to a favourable currency exchange rate. Political regulations may enhance organisations to do their businesses in other countries and some legal procedures may be introduced to support them. However, due to social or cultural factors, particular SMEs' products or services can be suitable mostly for the home country and offering them abroad would not bring expected profits.

The meso-level covers all the dimensions that are related with the industry/sector/market the company operates in. It includes the number of competitors, sources of competitive advantage, business networks, supply chains, market maturity and the number of potential customers. These factors make it possible to estimate potential incomes and the costs of running a business. The characteristics of these factors in a home country may impact international activity twofold. SMEs may not be interested in undertaking risks connected with internationalisation if there is a small number of competitors, the market is emerging and there is a high number of potential customers. They will be highly engaged in the home country market and the decision over entering other countries could be made after the home market shrinks. By contrast, negative circumstances may act as 'push' factors. SMEs that identified poor market potential in the home country may perceive entering foreign markets as the best way to leverage their businesses. Networks are also a very important factor which may create high operational potential, not only on the home country market but also in other countries. Being part of the network may help to set relationships with other companies and create foundations for cooperation in foreign countries.

The micro level refers to the characteristic of a particular company and encompasses internal factors. The SME sector is characterised as highly heterogenous. Thus, when analysing the context at the organisational level, such components as age, growth stage, product/service specificity, complexity of internal processes, managers/owners attitudes, and competences should be taken into account. The firm's age has an impact on market potential, the number of potential customers, brand recognition and resilience to potential threats. On the one hand, it can be stated that the older the firm, the better the recognition of the brand and experience in meeting customer expectations. Additionally, owners and managers of such companies have a higher awareness of their own resources and sources of competitive advantage. This may cause that decisions made and goals set are more thoughtful and embedded in market conditions. However, older firms may rely too strongly on their traditional way of thinking, which limits flexibility and adaptability. Additionally, with regard to customers, such companies may face a threat from new companies entering the market, which may be perceived as providing higher quality or lower prices.

The growth stage impacts short- and mid-term goals. Companies at the early stage in many cases strive to acquire customers to assure levels of income that will cover costs. Moreover, they do not have enough financial resources to conduct radical investments that would increase their market potential. Companies at the later stages in most cases have more resources which makes it possible to invest in the development of products/services or in activities aimed at entering new markets. In the decline stage, some organisations may find entering foreign markets to be a way to renewal, while others will not have enough resources to take any actions in this direction. Features of products/services directly correspond with the number and characteristics of customers. If a firm's offer is targeted to a wide range of customers, it is much easier to access them, but the company will surely face higher competition from other organisations. By contrast, niche products/services give the advantage of uniqueness but there are fewer potential customers. In this case, internationalisation can be a way to build a competitive position not only on the home country market.

The complexity of internal processes refers to their scope, number and level of detail. It defines the level of company autonomy in executing both key and supportive functions. Companies with advanced processes are more eager to analyse market data and respond to any changes relying on their own resources. The combination of the resources and processes (the way the resources are combined and used) creates dynamic capabilities (Eisenhardt & Martin, 2000). Advanced processes also help in building a competitive advantage based on quality and reliability. SMEs having complex internal processes are less dependent on business relationships with other companies when entering new markets. The manager/owner of the SME is a key person who defines the firm's strategic directions and makes decisions. The key features that should be taken into account are attitudes, knowledge, skills and business relationships. Attitudes are revealed in the approach to doing business and in some cases, internationalisation may be the aim of the owner from the very beginning. Knowledge and skills not only determine management efficiency but also help in entering foreign markets. In such a case, business networks or an ease in creating them will be supportive.

2.2.2 Contextual factors specific for international activity

It should be added that operating in the international context increases the complexity and unpredictability of the factors that may have an impact on enterprises. In the case of companies running their businesses on geographically diversified markets, they may focus and try to adjust to the home country context, the host country context or both. The particular approach strongly depends on the share of the outcomes of international operations in total revenues. This means that companies focus on the adjustment to the conditions of the markets that can potentially bring higher profits.

Research findings prove that there are some factors that are directly connected with international activity and have an impact on organisations that operate on foreign markets. According to research, the internal context (referring, e.g. to resource availability or managers' attitudes and competences) is more important, while other authors claim that it is the external context that is the most impactful (e.g.

networks or small psychic distance). However, it has been concluded in most studies that there is a combination of both internal and external factors that create the conditions under which companies operate.

In their article, Milliman et al. (1991) claimed that companies that run businesses on diverse markets have to deal not only with the cross-cultural environment but also with the cross-national environment, which includes social, legal and political settings. They also added that the degree of integration with these environments strongly relies on such factors as business model and strategy, structure and products/services. It can be concluded that all country-level factors are the primary factors which are analysed by companies that want to operate internationally and then these companies analyse whether they are able to adjust to these conditions.

According to Madsen and Servais (1997), the success of born-global companies depends on the following three main factors: conditions of the markets companies are entering; technological developments in the areas of production, transportation and communication; capabilities of people including the entrepreneur. The authors identified three categories of factors that have an impact on internationalisation success, these are as follows: founder – including past experience, ambition level, motivation; organisation – competence, routines, corporate governance structure; environment – market internationalisation, high/low technology, specialization.

A very similar categorisation of the contextual factors was presented by Hagen and Zucchella (2014). The authors enumerated the following categories of drivers for SME internationalisation: firms internal environment – resources (financial, technological), capabilities, networks, business idea and strategy; entrepreneurs' characteristics – international entrepreneurial orientation, global mindset, prior experience, learning; external environment – globalisation trends, ICT, industry-specific factors.

Boocock and Anderson (2003) claim that the success of SMEs operating on international markets may be highly dependent on the owner's motivation, the amount of capital available, the sources of information, pressures on the owner's–manager's time, competition from larger firms, and established network relationships. On the basis of the conducted research, they found that the following factors are important when analysing the internationalisation process: the potential size of the overseas markets, profit potential, similar customer needs, the opportunity to expand within the capabilities of the organisation, the scope and quality of relationships with existing domestic customers, the availability of foreign government assistance, the size of the domestic market, product/service quality and uniqueness, the attitudes and motivation of the owner/manager.

As mentioned before, SMEs have a very limited potential to shape the environment they operate in. Thus, the key factor that builds success might be the way firms acquire knowledge about foreign markets and adapt to new markets' conditions. According to Lu and Beamish (2001) knowledge and capabilities developed in the home market conditions may not be suitable in the new market. Access to relevant knowledge about the market is a factor that may impact the process of internationalisation, as operating on host country markets will require establishing legitimacy and building relationships with stakeholders on new markets. Taking the process of acquiring knowledge as a focal point in the research, Hillmerson and Johanson (2020) identified four categories of enterprises:

- Experiencers – incremental learning comes from own experiences
- Grafters – gaining knowledge by hiring new employees or acquiring other companies
- Networkers – using the generation of own experiences with the use of knowledge generated by other companies that are in the business network
- Pragmatists – companies that combine all sources of gathering information, including own experiences, hiring employees, acquiring other companies, and networking.

However, it should be noted that the descriptions of these types of organisations strongly refer to the firm's business model, age, stage of growth, owners' competences and business networks as well as to the market conditions and relationships between business partners that are already established. They are all interrelated with the factors discussed previously.

According to Bell et al. (2004), the following factors can be classified as environmental influencers: internal – firm resources, decision maker's characteristics, management competencies; domestic market conditions; international market conditions; industry/sector trends; globalization trends. However, the authors claimed that there is a difference between companies that are knowledge-intensive and those that operate traditionally. Organisations of the first type expand their markets more rapidly than traditional organisations and adapt a more proactive approach to internationalisation. These companies also create and develop products that could be marketed internationally. Knowledge-intensive firms are more likely to develop markets on the basis of relationships with customers and global industry trends. By contrast, traditional companies tend to choose markets that are geographically close or are perceived to have a small psychic distance (Bell et al., 2004).

Ruzzier et al. (2007) focused on the role of the SME owner's human capital in their research. They concluded that the following components play a crucial role in internationalisation: international business skills, international orientation, the perception of international risk, and management know-how. Thus, it can be stated that the level of these human capital components will strongly impact the decision of internationalisation regardless of other components.

The complexity of factors that should be taken into account when analysing the context of internationalising SMEs was presented by (Child et al., 2022). On the basis of a systematic literature review, the authors presented categories and detailed factors that were analysed and discussed in scientific papers between 2010 and 2020. All the factors were divided into *macro-level* – institutions and quasi-institutions, national culture, economic context, political context, industry; *meso-level* – networks/boundary spanning/collaboration, ownership/family firms, size of firms, temporal context (organisational learning and phases of internationalisation, technological context), and home-host country differences/similarities. Additionally, the authors demarcate some of the factors on those that may have a diverse shape in the host and home countries, e.g. there may exist *institutions and quasi-institutions* supporting international cooperation in the home or host country.

The dimensions and factors discussed above do not include all the elements that may create the environment of a particular SME. However, they cover those that differentiate the context most. It should also be added that some of these components should be analysed with regard to both home and host country conditions. For example, most *macro-level* factors create psychic distance between countries which may impact the decision on whether to enter a particular market. Similarly, the *meso-level* components in the host country may act as a pull factor for internationalisation, while the characteristics of these same components in the home country may be portrayed as a push factor, or when they are evaluated to be better in the home than in the host country, the company may decide to remain only the home country market. As mentioned at the beginning of this section, the number of context components and their potential characteristics make it impossible to generalise about the context and the term 'polycontextuality' should be used instead. This also results in the diversity of paths SMEs may potentially choose to internationalise.

2.3 Process of SME internationalisation

The concept of internationalisation has not been clearly defined, which results from its complexity and the difficulties of capturing its various aspects. The existent research on international business and management adopted various perspectives to analyse this phenomenon, inter alia, behavioural (Surdu et al., 2021), resource-based (Welch & Luostarinen, 1988; Ahokangas et al., 2010), dynamic capabilities (Luo, 2000; Prange & Verdier, 2011), knowledge-based (Mejri & Umemoto, 2010; Gulanowski et al., 2018), network (Johanson & Mattson, 1987; 2012), and entrepreneurial (Jones & Coviello, 2005; Ruzzier et al., 2006). Some scholars regard internationalisation as a strategy focused on company growth and building a competitive advantage (Attig et al., 2016), while others consider it as a process resulting from management innovations (Bilkey & Tesar, 1977; Cavusgil, 1980; Reid, 1981) or economic calculation relating to strategic market development (Buckley & Casson, 1999). In addition, there are conceptualisations that emphasise the role of learning in the company and using gradually acquired experiences on foreign markets (Johanson & Vahlne, 1990), the adaptation of the company's activities to foreign markets (Calof & Beamish; 1995), undertaking opportunistic (Melin, 1992) or entrepreneurial behaviours in recognising and exploiting market opportunities outside the home country (Jones & Coviello, 2005; Ruzzier et al., 2006).

In this book, the notion of internationalisation applies to the process in which 'a firm expands the sales of its goods or services across the borders of (...) countries into different geographic locations or markets' (Ayuso & Navarrete-Baez, 2018, p. 83) and becomes increasingly 'aware of the direct and indirect influence of international transactions' on its future activity (Coviello & McAuley, 1999, p. 225).

The first part of the above definition reflects our focus on the outward internationalisation, specifically such forms of international activity of a company that are targeted at customers in foreign markets. Thus, we exclude from our considerations the inward internationalisation, which applies to the development of foreign sourcing activities (Welch & Luostarinen, 1993, p. 44), and may either precede outward activities or accompany them. The second component of our definition emphasises the intra-organisational processes taking place in an internationalising company, in particular, the changes regarding its international orientation as well as the knowledge and capabilities needed for further activities. This, in turn, translates into adjusting the way it operates (Calof & Beamish, 1995, p. 116), including managing human resources, our primary concern.

As already mentioned, the internationalisation, even in its narrow sense as adopted in our definition, is a multifaceted phenomenon. Grasping the nature of this process goes beyond the scope of this book; therefore, our considerations address the most important aspects and dimensions that distinguish between different internationalisation pathways (Kuivalainen et al., 2012, p. 452). They include forms of international activity, the company's international experience, and the extent, scope and speed of internationalisation.

The forms of the international activity represent various methods of business organisation adopted by enterprises to either enter foreign markets or to continue expansion, thus some authors, including Young et al. (1989), and Jones and Young (2009), propose the term 'market entry and development modes', as more accurately reflecting their actual applications. We can distinguish three categories of these modes, namely exporting, collaboration and investment, which differ in the level of control, commitment and risk, as well as in terms of the nature of the rights and resources transferred (Anderson & Gatignon, 1986; Young et al., 1989; Jones & Young, 2009).

The least risky option that requires minimal capital commitment is export, which occurs either directly or indirectly through intermediaries from the domestic market. The former variant encompasses direct selling, running own sales offices in foreign markets, using overseas agents and distributors, and cooperating with a multinational that acts as an intermediator in the host country (Jones & Young, 2009, pp. 8–9). This provides the company with greater opportunities to gain international experience and influence the sales process abroad than the indirect form, which is associated with the problem of dependence on a domestic intermediary. The collaboration modes offer more opportunities for establishing synergistic relationships, reducing costs and risks, and learning from foreign partners; however, this requires greater commitment than exporting. This category encompasses diverse forms of temporary cross-border cooperation, such as industry consortium, contract management, licencing, franchising and strategic alliances (Inkpen, 2005, p. 404; Jones & Young, 2009, p. 8). The last group of entry modes are foreign direct investments, also called equity modes, which comprise joint ventures and wholly owned subsidiaries, formed either as greenfield or brownfield ventures (acquired businesses or mergers). Their common features are high entry costs, a high level of capital commitment and control exercised by the firm. However, in the case of a joint venture, the scope of control as well as the risk distributed among the partners depends on their capital commitment. The advantages of these modes over the previous categories are the opportunity to gain diverse international experience and the direct impact on shaping the company's image in the host countries as well as building relationships with customers and other stakeholders.

The international experience of a company is usually defined as the duration of its presence in host countries (Mohr et al., 2014; Mohr & Batsakis, 2017) regardless of the form of outward international activity. In the case of SMEs, it applies to the period since the firm started exporting on a consistent basis (Contractor et al., 2005, p. 91). Regardless the size of the company, expanding operations beyond the domestic country is associated with additional costs, recognised in IB studies as the liabilities of foreignness (LoF) (Hymer, 1960/1976; Zaheer, 1995). Amongst various sources of LoF, the unfamiliarity with the foreign environment constitutes one of most relevant obstacles (Zaheer, 1995; Bell et al., 2012). Thus, it takes time for a company to reduce LoF through accumulated knowledge and exposure to internationalisation-related challenges (Hymer, 1960/1976; Zaheer & Mosakowski, 1997; Tan et al., 2007). Owing to a longer presence in foreign markets, such a company also gains an additional advantage on the domestic market based on foreign expertise resulting from the exporting-related challenges and experience in competing with foreign/international rivals (Leonidou et al., 2007, p. 744). Importantly, the mere length of time might be misleading or at least an insufficient indicator of international experience, especially from the perspective of accumulated knowledge on foreign markets and cross-border operations. The quality of such an experience may vary depending on the differentiation of overseas markets and the nature of the company's international activities. In other words, being present in a direct manner at various locations on a consistent three-year basis may result in richer experiential knowledge with a greater potential applicability in further expansion when compared to occasionally selling products or services via intermediaries over several decades.

The extent of internalisation represents another important aspect of this phenomenon. As Øyna and Alon (2018, p. 162) found in their literature review, the term 'extent' (or 'the scale', as proposed by Kuivalainen et al., 2012, p. 454) most often applies to the intensity of international activity and is measured as a foreign-sales-to-total-sales ratio (FSTS).[1] The combination of the above ratio and the propensity to internationalise, indicating whether an SME derives part of its sales from exporting, reflects another widely used construct, namely international commitment (Fernandez & Nieto, 2006; Martineau & Pastoriza, 2016). This provides us with the additional, yet relevant information on the nature of an enterprise's exposure to challenges involved in this process. Interestingly, the proportion of foreign sales to total sales also serves as a 'surrogate measure to capture the effectiveness of international performance' (Zhou, 2007, p. 287).

The scope, as a dimension of internationalisation, denotes international or global diversity, which either refers to the number of international markets entered, or to the geographical spread of these markets (Øyna & Alon, 2018, p. 162). In case of the latter, the scope can be regarded as a measure reflecting market strategies ranging from concentration to market diversification (Ayal & Zif, 1979; Kuivalainen et al., 2007). A distinct construct that may refer to the spatial dimension of internationalisation directly (e.g. Shoham et al., 1995) or indirectly (e.g. Klein & Roth, 1990) is the distance that reflects the differences (their actual or subjective perception in the case of psychic distance) between home and host country.[2] This concept is firmly embedded in the stage approach to internationalisation (i.e. internationalisation process theories), where it is assumed that companies initially explore relatively close markets and with increasing experience, enter more distant markets (Johanson & Vahlne, 1977, 1990, 2009).

Speed, as Johanson and Kalinic (2016, p. 829) accurately noticed, generally denotes the distance travelled divided by the time taken to travel it; however, in the context of internationalisation, it is understood in a metaphorical way. Moreover, as Hilmersson et al. (2017, p. 23) found 'different measures are used to represent the same concepts, and in other cases, the same measures are used to represent different concepts', e.g. pace (Vermeulen & Barkema, 2002; Zhou, 2007; Lin, 2012), earliness (Zhou & Wu, 2014; Freixanet & Renart, 2020), precocity (Zucchella et al., 2007; Kuivalainen et al., 2012), rapidity (Bell et al., 2001; Freeman et al., 2006), and acceleration (Pla-Barber & Escribá-Esteve, 2006; Weerawardena et al., 2007).

Despite the abundance of the above terminology, we can consider two fundamentally different contexts that determine the understanding of the concept of speed. One concerns the initial stages of internationalisation and relatively small businesses, where it serves to distinguish between early and late internationalisers, while the other applies to large companies that conduct their overseas activities in various forms (modes). In the first situation, the measurement of speed focuses on the period from the inception of an enterprise to the start of its internationalisation (Øyna & Alon, 2018, p. 162). More specifically, the speed of this process reflects the progress in which a young company "obtains 'a substantial proportion of total revenue' from the sale of outputs in multiple countries" (Zhou, 2007, p. 287). The earliness and the precocity of internationalisation can be regarded as the semantically closest categories that apply to this context. In the case of large MNCs, the speed is considered rather as the pace of post-entry expansion. Thus, it can be measured as the average number of foreign outlets divided by the number of years since the firm's first entry to the international market (Chang and Rhee 2011; Chetty et al., 2014; Mohr & Batsakis, 2017), or similarly as 'the cumulative number of new countries that the firm has entered through FDI as of a given year divided by the number of years elapsed since it entered the first foreign country' (García-García et al., 2017, p. 97).

Considerable initial interest in the internationalisation of large companies dates back to the 1950s and 1960s, when various economic theories emerged, e.g. the internalisation theory, the transaction cost theory, the eclectic paradigm, and the monopolistic advantage theory. However, research focused on SME internationalisation appeared much later, in the 1970s (Ruzzier et al., 2006, pp. 480–482). In this case, theoretical foundations were derived from a different background, more specifically, the behavioural theory of the company (Cyert & March, 1963) and Penrose's theory of firms' growth (Penrose, 1959). These different roots of research development reflect the specificity of SME internationalisation; moreover, distinctive features of these entities render a number of theories developed for the multinationals inapplicable in a small business setting. However, this does not apply to the internationalisation process theories (i.e. the Uppsala model by Johanson & Vahlne, 1977, 1990, 2009) and the innovation-related models developed, inter alia, by Bilkey & Tesar, (1977) and Cavusgil (1980). They posit that along with the gained international experience and participation in networks dispersed in various locations, enterprises develop their international activity gradually, i.e. they increase the scope, distance (physical and psychic) that separates target markets from the home market and involvement in these markets (from occasional exporting to diverse entry modes, including equity based). It should be noted, however, that in reality, the growth phases of internationalisation may alternate with periods of decreasing and re-increasing international commitment to foreign markets (Dominguez & Mayrhofer, 2017). An example of deviation from incremental internationalisation occurring in the context of SMEs are the companies named born-again global (BAGs). After a long period of activity in their home country, BAGs suddenly begin to internationalise because of critical events (e.g. a change in ownership, acquisition by another firm, or international expansion initiated by key domestic customer) that trigger a rapid shift of the managerial focus from domestic to international markets (Bell et al., 2001, 2003). In addition to BAGs, there are a considerable number of small and medium-sized businesses involved in internationally dispersed activities almost immediately since their inception. This phenomenon of early and rapidly internationalising SMEs is at the core of the International New Venture/Born Global (INV/BG) theory (Oviatt & McDougall, 1994; 2005; Knight & Cavusgil 1996; 2004), which receives more attention in the next subchapter.

The uniqueness of SME internationalisation stems from limited human, financial, technological and information resources (Steinhäuser et al., 2021; Lobo et al., 2020). Compared to large companies, they are much more sensitive to their external environment and quicker in responding to institutional pressures (Lobo et al., 2020). On the one hand, they demonstrate greater entrepreneurial dynamism, quick decision-making, and flexibility (Paul et al., 2017; Steinhäuser et al., 2021) that propel their growth in the international market. On the other, their liabilities of smallness (Kuivalainen et al., 2012; Paul et al., 2017; Chandra et al., 2020), fragile structures and insufficient knowledge of target markets limit their commitment to internationalisation, which is less than that of large companies (Cheng & Yu, 2008; Steinhäuser et al., 2021). Thus, the predominant form of their international activity is exporting (Leonidou et al., 2007; Kuivalainen et al., 2012) and online presence/sales in foreign markets (Pezderka & Sinkowics, 2011; Sinkowics et al., 2013), while equity-based modes such as partially or wholly owned subsidiaries are much less often used. For the same reasons, as discussed above, SMEs heavily rely upon their networks (Paul et al., 2017) and reach for collaborative modes along with their international expansion more frequently than multinationals (Musteen et al., 2014; Bruneel & De Cock, 2016).

SMEs also differ from large companies in terms of the individual, organisational and environmental factors affecting internationalisation in its pre-entry and post-entry phases. Table 2.1 compiles the determinants of SME internationalisation, which are organised according to the above-mentioned categories of factors. Importantly, these factors can be also considered in terms of the proactive or reactive nature of their influence. The proactive impact relates to an enterprise's interest in exploiting either organisational competences or emerging foreign market opportunities (e.g. the interest to expand abroad and the possession of networks or knowledge advantages over competitors in the target market), while the reactive denotes pressures (e.g. increasing competition, saturation of domestic market) that require a response from this company (Leonidou et al., 2007).

Table 2.1 Determinants of SME internationalisation

Level	Kuivalainen et al. (2012)	Francioni, Pagano & Castellani (2016)	Steinhäuser et al. (2021)	Martineau & Pastoriza (2016)
	Determinants of early and late internationalisation	Drivers of exporting	Determinants of internationalisation in general	Determinants of international commitment (early internationalisation excluded)
Individual	• Managerial mindset • Previous experience • Entrepreneurial orientation	• Interest, competences, and skills • Personality/subjective characteristics* • Socio-demographic factors* (age, gender, nationality, family membership)	• Personal and professional networks • International experience • International orientation • International opportunities recognition • Knowledge domain of the firm	• Previous professional and personal international experience • Attitudes and perceptions towards foreign markets
Organisational	• Resources • Knowledge • Strategic orientation • Network • Capabilities • Liabilities (of smallness, foreignness, newness) • Learning the advantages of newness (in early internationalisation)	• HR management procedures* • R & D, innovation and productivity (possession of proprietary technical knowledge; product innovation; process innovation*) • Marketing and sales (marketing capabilities; Internet/web marketing*) • Purchasing (international sourcing experience*)	• Firm structure • Firm capabilities • International orientation • International opportunities recognition • Knowledge domain	• Size • Network with suppliers, customers, government agencies, key foreign actors • Product innovation capacity

(Continued)

Table 2.1 (Continued)

Environmental	• Industry factors, • Environmental dynamism, uncertainty, turbulence • Other aspects of environment (customers, technology, competition, regulatory) • Distance (home versus host countries) • Country of origin	• Home country (saturation/shrinkage of domestic market; need to reduce dependence/risk of domestic market; export promotion programs) • Host country (identification of better opportunities abroad; potential for extra growth; potential for extra sales/profits; close physical proximity to foreign markets) • Network (personal networks* ; business networks including customers* and intermediaries*)	• Domestic uncertainties	• Government export programs • Home-country market difficulties

Note

* Emerging drivers that require further research suggested in the review by Francioni et al. (2016).

As Leonidou et al. (2007, p. 737) found, SMEs driven by internal (individual and organisational) factors 'have been described as more objective-oriented in their export behaviour, compared to those stimulated by external factors'. They also observed that a strategic orientation in exporting occurs in enterprises with a more proactive stimulation, while companies responding to pressures adopt an opportunistic and passive approach.

Undoubtedly, SMEs are driven by a configuration of various stimuli when entering foreign markets; nonetheless, the relative importance of these factors and the content of the initial set change with time (Kuivalainen et al., 2012; Hagen & Zucchella, 2014). At the pre-entry and initial stage of international expansion, the characteristics of the entrepreneurs/top management team are of key importance, since they act as initiators, decision-makers, and strategists; they also provide the organisation with resources necessary for operation and are the main source of human and relational capital. These issues are even more crucial in SMEs that internationalise early and rapidly (Zucchella et al., 2007; Kuivalainen et al., 2012). With time, however, the organisational determinants become more relevant, not only for the selection of entry modes (Bruneel & De Cock, 2016) but also in other aspects of the gradual (Martineau & Pastoriza, 2016) and accelerated internationalisation strategies (Romanello & Chiarvesio, 2017; Breuillot, 2021) as well as in the case of non-linear pathways (Steinhäuser et al., 2021). Furthermore, their contribution can be essential for the long-term survival of these companies (Efrat & Shoham, 2012).

2.4 Characteristics of early internationalised small and medium firms

Early and rapid (accelerated) internationalisation has been recognised as a specific behavioural pattern followed by small and medium enterprises (Kuivalainen et al., 2012, p. 450) the distinctive feature of which is a very short period preceding their involvement in international operations, most often up to three years from their inception (Rialp et al., 2005; Zucchella et al., 2007; Knight & Liesch, 2016; Romanello & Chiarvesio, 2019). The research interest in early internationalised firms (EIFs) dates back to the late 1980s (Knight & Liesch, 2016, p. 96) and has increased exponentially since then. Along with this growth, several terms have emerged to denote companies that internationalised at their formation or shortly thereafter. These include rapidly internationalising ventures (Cesinger et al., 2012); born globals (Rennie; 1993; Knight & Cavusgil, 1996; Madsen & Servais, 1997); international new ventures (Oviatt & McDougall, 1994); global start-ups (Oviatt & McDougall, 1994, 2005); true born globals (Kuivalainen et al., 2007); born internationals (Kundu & Katz, 2003; Johanson & Martín Martín, 2015); born regionals (Lopez et al., 2009; Baum et al., 2015); instant internationals (Dana, 2001); innate exporters (Ganitsky, 1989); instant exporters (McAuley, 1999).

Recent literature reviews (e.g. Knight & Liesch, 2016; Øyna, & Alon, 2018; Romanello & Chiarvesio, 2019) suggest the predominance of two notions, namely born globals (BGs) and international new ventures (INVs), used either interchangeably, jointly or separately. The former was introduced by Rennie (1993) in the context of young Australian exporting firms with a substantial proportion of foreign sales and further adopted by Knight and Cavusgil (1996, 2004). Initially, Knight and Cavusgil (1996) characterised BGs as 'small, technology-oriented companies that operate in the international markets from the earliest days of their establishment' (p. 11), of which the most distinguishing feature is being 'managed by entrepreneurial visionaries who view the world as a single, borderless marketplace from the time of the firm's founding' (p. 12). However, the most acknowledged definition derives from their seminal paper published in 2004, from which we can learn that born globals are 'entrepreneurial startups that, from or near their founding, seek to derive a substantial proportion of their revenue from the sales of products in international markets' (Knight & Cavusgil, 2004, p. 124). The second most prominent concept (INVs) applies to 'business organisations that, from inception, seek to derive significant competitive advantage from the use of resources and the sales of outputs in multiple countries' (Oviatt & McDougall, 1994, p. 49).

The common component of the above definitions constitutes the relevance of sales in multiple countries initiated at or shortly after the inception of an enterprise, while the difference between them relates to inward internationalisation (sourcing) included only in the concept of INVs. Moreover, as noted by Ferguson et al. (2021), BGs are entirely new firms by definition, whereas INVs may also emerge as a spinout from an existing company, thus they consider the former as a subcategory of the latter. This attempt to associate both concepts refers to the original taxonomy of INVs based on the number of value chain activities they coordinate and the number of countries they have entered (Oviatt & McDougall, 2005, p. 37). More specifically, Oviatt and McDougall (1994, 2005) distinguished: (1) enterprises that coordinate just a few cross-border activities that can be either export/import start-ups or multinational traders, depending on the number of countries the operate in; (2) ventures involved in more extensive co-ordination that differ in terms of the geographical scope, i.e. geographically-focused and global start-ups. Ferguson et al. (2021) suggest that global start-ups in papers by Oviatt & McDougall (1994, 2005) are the equivalent of the born-global-firm concept by Knight & Cavusgil (2004), although this view is not widely acknowledged.

As far as the scope is concerned, some scholars emphasise the relevance and/or practical applicability of this aspect when considering differentiation among born globals or EIFs in general (e.g. Kundu & Katz, 2003; Chetty & Campbell-Hunt, 2004; Kuivalainen et al, 2007; Cesinger et al., 2012). They argue that incorporating this dimension into empirical research allows distinguishing between regional and global patterns, and thus more accurately reflects the real behaviours of rapidly internationalising SMEs (Lopez et al., 2009; Baum et al., 2015).

In summing up, we must agree with the conclusion by Knight and Liesch (2016, p. 94) that the attempts to delineate the boundaries of these concepts did not bring forth a sufficiently clear and widely accepted differentiation. Thus, various researchers opt for using them jointly (e.g. Cesinger et al, 2012; Romanello & Chiarvesio, 2019; Jiang et al., 2020) or even interchangeably (e.g. Hennart, 2014; Øyna, & Alon, 2018). Consequently, when discussing early internationalised firms, we derive from both streams of research and focus on the features that distinguish EIFs from other internationalisers.

Since the nature of EIFs appears complex and multifaceted, researchers apply various theoretical perspectives to grasp the specifics of these firms and factors underlying the accelerated internationalisation, inter alia (Øyna, & Alon, 2018; Jiang et al., 2020):

- A resource-based view that considers the idiosyncratic bundle of resources, such as specialised knowledge, innovative, and unique products, as enablers and facilitators of entering foreign markets and successfully competing regardless of their constraints (liabilities of smallness, newness, and foreignness).
- A view of dynamic capabilities that highlights the contribution of various organisational capabilities to international expansion, e.g. firm innovation, technology, marketing and learning.
- A network perspective that emphasises the benefits of networking, alliances, and social capital in developing business and expanding beyond the domestic market, including risk and cost reduction,

better access to international opportunities and various resources
that would otherwise be insufficient or unavailable.

- Entrepreneurship theories and an opportunity-based view that
focus on entrepreneurial characteristics (especially, innovation,
risk-taking and proactiveness) as well as opportunity identification
and exploitation are regarded as fundamental factors determining
internationalisation.

However, until now, the portrait of early internationalised firms
emerging from the empirical studies has remained incomplete and
fragmented, partially due to their narrow theoretical underpinnings
limited to particular perspectives and inconsistent operational definitions of EIFs that hamper the comparison and integration of
findings from various pieces of research. On the other hand, we
observe relentless pursuits to grasp the nature of accelerated internationalisation in conceptual works that brought forth various
theoretical models (Table 2.2). Some of them have been empirically
verified (e.g. Zucchella et al., 2007; Efrat & Shoham, 2012),
while others represent an outcome of extensive literature reviews
(e.g. Rialp et al., 2005; Jiang et al., 2020).

Based on models shown in Table 2.2 and recent literature reviews
(Cesinger et al., 2012; Chandra et al., 2012; Knight & Liesch, 2016;
Dzikowski, 2018; Øyna, & Alon, 2018; Paul & Rosado-Serrano,
2019; Romanello & Chiarvesio, 2019; Jiang et al., 2020), we can
identify several characteristics of EIFs with respect to which the
findings are fairly consistent. Firstly, the basic feature that distinguishes them from other internationalisers is the timing and speed of
internationalisation, which involves simultaneous entry into various
markets regardless of their physical or psychic proximity. Some
scholars also suggest that differences in a firm's behaviour between
EIFs and slow (late) internationalisers persist in the later phases of
international expansion (Gabrielsson et al., 2008; Sleuwaegen &
Onkelinx, 2014; Romanello & Chiarvesio, 2017); however, these issues have not yet been sufficiently explored (Ciszewska-Mlinarič
et al., 2020, p. 451). Secondly, EIFs are entrepreneurial companies
that are capable of developing and exploiting opportunities and have
demonstrated a global (or at least international) focus from the
earliest time of their existence. Thirdly, they adopt a proactive approach to internationalisation and operate in a highly flexible
manner. This implies the usage of various entry modes with a predominance of non-equity forms and a stronger preference for cooperative modes compared to late (slow) internationalisers (Schwens

Table 2.2 Features and determinants of early internationalised small and medium firms in the selected conceptual frameworks or models

	Madsen & Servais (1997)	Rialp et al. (2005)**	Weerawardena et al. (2007)**	Zucchella et al. (2007)	Efrat & Shoham (2012)	Jiang et al. (2020)
Key characteristics	Research model of BGs focused on antecedences of propensity to internationalise and further develop	Research model of EIFs (precocity, speed, extent, scope, forms of international activity, sustainable superior international performance)	Research model of BG internationalisation (speed, extent, scope)	Research model focused on drivers of EIFs (precocity), tested empirically	Research model focused on determinants of: a Strategic short-term performance, b Survival of BGs in a five-year-term tested empirically	Conceptual framework focused on determinants of EIFs (propensity, speed, extent, scope), their general (international) and performance outcomes
Individual	• Founder's prior experience (international, product-related) • Motivation • Ambition level	Entrepreneurs'/managers' human capital comprising: • Characteristics • Ties • Roles	Owner/manager profile • International entrepreneurial orientation • Global mindset • Prior international experience • Learning orientation	• Entrepreneur's education • Foreign languages* • International experience* • Prior work experience in family business*	n/a	• Values and perceptions of founder(s) • Characteristics of founder(s)

(Continued)

Table 2.2 (Continued)

Organisational					
• Competence (specialised, niche-oriented) and routines (experience-based) • Corporate governance (composition of the board members and their backgrounds) • Structure (hybrid forms of governance structures in their export channels)	Intangible resources of structural capital • Technological capital • Organisational capital • Relational capitalFirm-specific international capability conditioned by human and structural capital and based upon: • Specialised knowledge management and learning processes (know-how) • Exploitation of core competencies • Internationally oriented routines • Lack of domestic path dependencies • Absorptive capacity	Distinctive capabilities • Market-focused learning capability (market information) • Internally focused learning capability (technological and non-technological) • Networking capability (knowledge acquisition and developing complementary resources) Factors conditioned by the above capabilities • Superior marketing capability (ability to position the firm rapidly in the global niche markets) • Knowledge-intensive products	• Focalisation of strategy (niche positioning)*	• Technological/ R&D capability (b)* • Capability of developing market knowledge (a)* • Capability of active measurement of marketing effectiveness (b) • Management capabilities (b)*	• Strategy • Entrepreneurial orientation • Firm characteristics and competences (size, technology, relational resources, financial capital, organisation structure and system)

| Environmental | • Market internationalisation and specialisation,
• High technology industry | • Type of sector (high/low tech, manufacturing/services)
• Geographic context (country, rural/urban area, industrial districts)
• Local and international networks | n/a | • Inter-organisational networks (formal/social inter-firm agreements; knowledge sharing)
• Location specifics (industrial district or cluster) | • High-growth foreign markets (a)*
• Highly technological turbulent markets (a)*
• High-risk target countries – negative impact (a)*, (b)* | • Industry characteristics (internationalisation, knowledge/technological intensity, dynamism, hostility)
• Domestic and international market (size, potential, internationalisation)
• Geographic location (cluster dynamism, competition for resources) |

Notes

* Tested by the authors of a given model in their empirical studies and statistically significant.

** These models regard the individual characteristics as factors influencing organisational attributes listed in this table.

& Kabst, 2009). Fourthly, while entering foreign markets, these enterprises are young and small, thus their market experience is minimal and the resources are very limited. Therefore, their growth initially relies heavily upon knowledge, skills and other resources contributed by their founders. However, the key decision-makers at EIFs, unlike their counterparts in late (slow) internationalisers, tend to have prior international experience, internationalisation-related motivation and aspirations and well-established international networks. These attributes contribute to the development of crucial organisational capabilities, enable these entrepreneurs to quickly expand their businesses abroad, and determine the selection of markets and network partners.

EIFs literature also suggests that these companies tend to adopt specific business models and strategies that are focused on value creation through product differentiation, technological innovativeness or product design, which are aimed at niche markets and/or standardised and highly specialised products offered to a specific group of customers internationally dispersed using low-cost information and delivery methods (Rialp et al., 2005; Zucchella et al., 2007; Hennart, 2014, Paul & Rosado-Serrano, 2019; Jiang et al., 2020). Such a strategic choice accompanied by network relationships based on mutual trust (Freeman et al., 2010; Fernhaber & Li, 2013; Hagen & Zucchella, 2014;) enables them to successfully compete in high-growth markets, regardless of their limited experience and size (Efrat & Shoham, 2012; Cannone & Ughetto, 2014; Paul & Rosado-Serrano, 2019). Some of these constraints, and more specifically, the lack of experience prior to entering foreign markets, are also regarded as a distinctive strength of EIFs compared to other internationalisers, and have been conceptualised by Autio et al. (2000) and Zahra (2005) as the learning advantage of newness. Nonetheless, the actual contribution of this feature to accelerated internationalisation seems more nuanced,[3] thus further research is required to address the above controversies (De Clercq et al., 2012), not to mention other inconsistencies and gaps in the extant knowledge on EIFs.

What undoubtedly hinders any attempts to systematize and integrate knowledge about these companies is the lack of consensus on the operation definition of EIFs. In this dispute, some scholars (e.g. Romanello & Chiarvesio, 2019) strongly opt for a unified definition derived from Knight and Causvil (2004) based on the maximum threshold of a three-year period from inception to the beginning of international operation combined with the required share of foreign sales, i.e. at least 25% of total sales. Others more cautiously confirm that this operationalisation is most widely used in this context (e.g. Kuivalainen et al., 2012; Knight & Liesch, 2016; Øyna, & Alon, 2018). The common argument underlying the above stance is the further advancement of empirical-based knowledge conditioned by a consistent definition EIFs, which is a prerequisite for comparing and integrating findings from various research settings. Finally, some scholars (e.g. Cesinger et al., 2012) propose a relativistic approach by claiming that 'employing a single definition in empirical studies across contexts is dysfunctional' (p. 1835). They justify this relativism by the occurrence of different interpretations of the early and rapid internationalisation depending on the location of research in Europe or the US.

Having acknowledged the controversies on a universal operational definition, we felt that our study would contribute more to the advancement of knowledge about EIFs if we adopted the aforementioned definition by Knight and Cavusgil (2004). Either way, due to the focus of this book, an even more challenging aspect of research on the accelerated internationalisation of SMEs is the paucity of empirical-based knowledge on their activities, outcomes, and determinants in phases other than the pre-entry and entry of this process. These issues constitute an important background for our discussion of HRM-related challenges that we take up in the third chapter (Section 3.3).

Notes

1 It should be noted that some authors use another term, the degree of internationalisation, measured in the same way (e.g. De Clercq et al., 2005; Cesinger et al., 2012).
2 Alternative ways of operationalising distance are based on measuring cultural or institutional differences between the considered countries (Stöttinger & Schlegelmilch, 1998; Brewer, 2007; Kuivalainen et al., 2007).
3 This advantage of newness supposedly consists in more rapid and effective learning from foreign activities without the burden of the past (domestic) routines (Aspelund et al., 2007, p. 1442). However, other scholars point at the paradoxical role of this experience and the uncertain final result. More specifically, EIFs can benefit from learning that is unbiased by the past and at the same time, their learning may be more challenging/less effective due to the insufficient absorptive capacity based upon pre-existing knowledge (De Clercq et al., 2012, p. 163).

3 HRM-related challenges faced by internationalised SMEs

3.1 The specificity of human resource management in SMEs

The specificity of human resource management (HRM) in early internationalised small and medium firms stems from the nature of the internationalisation process and the characteristics of human resource management in SMEs. The first issue was discussed in the previous chapter, thus we will focus here on identifying the typical features of HRM in SMEs.

The growing interest in the functioning of small- and medium-sized firms that we have observed for the last few decades is due to their increasing importance in the economies of many countries. Such firms account for more than 99% of enterprises in the European Union, OECD, or G20 countries and they employ more than half of all employees and significantly contribute to the creation of added value (OECD, 2015; European Commission, 2017). Despite the great internal diversity of enterprises classified as small- and medium-sized, they show some common features that allow them to be distinguished from large companies. It is worth mentioning here that small- and medium-sized enterprises are defined by quantitative and qualitative criteria, while the definitions themselves may differ from country to country (Festing et al., 2017; Daszkiewicz & Wach, 2013). The common characteristics of small- and medium-sized firms most frequently mentioned in the literature include limited resources, fewer customers and markets, centralised management, the owner–manager union, flat and flexible structures, the propensity for reactive actions, informal, dynamic operating strategies, and specific contexts (Festing et al., 2017; Pauli, 2018; Daszkiewicz & Wach, 2013). It is worth emphasising here that small- and medium-sized enterprises are not miniaturisations of large enterprises (Storey, 1994), which means that

DOI: 10.4324/9781003319979-3

their specificities, problems and practices should not be understood as reduced versions of those found in large enterprises (Ates et al., 2013). Similarly, the methodology of their study should not be a copy of the methods and tools used in the study of large organisations as it requires a different approach (Strużyna, 2002).

The above-presented characteristics of small and medium enterprises determine their human resources management policies and practices. At the outset, it is worth noting that in many publications devoted to the issue of entrepreneurship and the functioning of small- and medium-sized enterprises, relatively less space is devoted to issues related to employment, the formation of labour relations, and human resource management compared to other areas such as finance, law, or marketing, and in some of them, this aspect is even omitted (Sidor-Rządkowska, 2010; Wapshott & Mallett, 2016). This is somewhat of a paradox as in many such companies, human capital is the main source of competitiveness. Consequently, human resource management is very significant but is sometimes practiced at a lower level compared to large companies (Moš, 2017). Meanwhile, the SME sector is the place of employment for many people who consciously make such a choice in the belief that they will receive better working conditions there, as well as more flexibility, less formalised processes, and higher job satisfaction as a result.

The growing importance of SMEs in the economy and the large share of employment in such companies are factors influencing the undertaking of research on HR issues and the increase in the number of HRM publications on this topic. The literature produced in recent years has quite commonly highlighted a different approach to people management in small- and medium-sized enterprises compared to large organisations (Raby & Gilman, 2012; Festing et al., 2017; Pauli, 2018). Although the range of practices may be similar to those found in large organisations, the way they are implemented and delivered will be different. It is also important to remember that small- and medium-sized enterprises are not a homogeneous category (Wapshott & Mallett, 2016).

With regard to the number of employees, which significantly affects the architecture of the human resource management system, among the listed companies we find micro-, small-, and medium-sized enterprises. Generally, an increase in the number of employees leads to the greater formalisation of HRM (Moš, 2017). The diversity of approaches to HRM in these enterprises results from the specificity of the industry, the technologies used, cultural conditions and other factors forming the internal and external context of their functioning. A characteristic feature of human resource management in SMEs is the dominant role of the owner–manager, determining personnel decisions taken in both the short term and the long term. The level of awareness of owner–managers about the importance of capital and its place in the company's business model determines the approach to HRM and the practices applied in this area. Another frequently indicated feature of the approach to HRM in SMEs is the lower degree of formalisation and the use of simplified procedures and tools (Sidor-Rządkowska, 2010; Wapshott & Mallett, 2016; Festing et al., 2017). HR processes are most often implemented in a centralised manner by owner–managers, with no or limited support from HR professionals due to the lack of such organisational units or limited cooperation with consulting firms. Numerous publications on human resource management in small- and medium-sized firms address both individual aspects and the whole process. Based on their analysis of publications produced in the last 25 years, Harney and Alkhalaf (2020) mapped the following research areas in this field: definitional para-meters, the nature of HRM practices, the impact of HRM practices on the performance of SMEs, and the key determinants of HRM within the context of SMEs.

Small- and medium-sized enterprises are defined differently in dif-ferent countries. The criterion often used for the division is the number of employees, which is important from the point of view of employment and people management. For example, in the United States, the SME category includes companies employing up to 500 people. In the European Union countries, this category includes companies employing up to 250 people (Harney & Alkhalaf, 2020). Within this group, a dis-tinction is made between micro-, small-, and medium-sized firms, the distinction of which is an important issue in the study of human resource management practices and the factors that determine them. Determining the specificity of human resource management also requires considering qualitative criteria such as newness, smallness, ambition, and growth, which determine the actions taken in the area of HRM (Harney, 2021). Similarly, taking into account the stage of development of a given company provides a better insight into typical employment challenges and HRM interventions (Krishnan & Scullion, 2017).

HRM practices in SMEs, which are the subject of many studies, are presented both as a bundle of practices and in the form of individual practices. The most frequently described human resources management practices in SMEs are those belonging to basic HR functions, in parti-cular: recruitment and selection, training and development, remunera-tion, motivation, appraisal, and staff turnover (Sidor-Rządkowska, 2010; Wapshott & Mallett, 2016). In addition to the above practices belonging to the basic canon of HRM, the subject of the study are also other practices related to employee relations, communication, health and safety, work-life balance (Harney & Alkhalaf, 2020) and the issues of agile and resilient HRM undertaken in recent years (Heilmann et al., 2020) as well as green HRM (O'Donohue & Torugsa, 2016). With reference to the characteristics of management in SMEs presented earlier, it can be concluded that in general, HRM practices are informal in these companies. They take place in a reactive manner, emerging from contextual conditions, and they are the opposite of the coherent bundles of HRM practices in large organisations. Proposals found in the literature to conceptualise the diverse HRM practices in SMEs and their clustering include both the traditional view referring to the core HR functions as well as other ways of configuring them, e.g. through clustering (Festing et al., 2017; Pocztowski et al., 2021).

The issue of the impact of HRM practices on the performance of SMEs is an important area of research and practitioners' interest. The relationship between HRM and performance is captured both as the impact of the bundles of practices on performance and as the impact of single practices on it (Sheehan, 2014; Harney & Alkhalaf, 2020). As is well known, performance in general and the performance of SMEs are multidimensional constructs and can include different types of HRM outcomes, e.g. business, organisational, and HR-related outcomes (Pocztowski et al., 2021). Most of the studies and resulting publications include various contextualised subjective measures of performance, such as revenue growth, sales level, profitability, innovation, export orientation, customer number and satisfaction, entrepreneurial orientation, organisational ambidexterity, employee commitment and satisfaction, labour cost and productivity, employee retention and turnover (Harney & Alkhalaf, 2020). It can be concluded that research results confirm the positive relationship between the activities undertaken within the framework of HRM and performance and some authors suggest that this relationship is stronger in SMEs than in large companies (Rauch & Hatak, 2016). Research also indicates the existence of associations between individual HRM practices and certain performance indicators: increased profitability, innovation and lower labour turnover. In addition to the importance of individual practices, the positive impact of the bundles of practices on the performance of SMEs has also been confirmed (Sheehan, 2014). It is worth noting at this point that there is a kind of evolution in the perception and study of the relationship between HRM practices and the performance of SMEs. This involves moving away from the initially applied universal 'best practice' approach towards considering this relationship in a broader context of the functioning of SMEs and considering a series of independent variables that determine the performance of SMEs.

Human resource management in general, and in SMEs in particular, always takes place in a specific context which is formed by internal and external factors that determine the application of specific HRM practices. The literature has emphasised particularly strongly in recent years the need to also consider context in research on HRM (Cooke, 2018; Mayrhofer et al. 2018). These issues are discussed in more detail in the previous chapter, thus we will limit ourselves here to the conclusions drawn from the review of research on HRM in SMEs. In general, it can be concluded that contextual factors are taken into account in part of them to determine the level and specificity of HRM practices used. Among the internal factors of particular relevance to HRM practices, the following are considered most frequently: size, age, resources, ownership, capital intensity, and HR specialisation. As for the external factors, the following are most often included: industry sector, labour market, institutional factors, trade unions, value chain/networks and internationalisation (Harney & Alkhalaf, 2020). Referring to the general characteristics of SMEs presented earlier, it can be emphasised here that contextual factors significantly determine the approach to HRM in SMEs, e.g. the timing of the introduction of certain HRM practices or the use of certain other practices (Pocztowski & Pauli, 2022). Often, these are specific internal or external events, such as ownership changes, succession, hiring a professional manager, increased pressure from competitors, the deterioration of economic performance, problems with access to talented employees, and crisis situations, e.g. those related to the Covid-19 pandemic.

As mentioned earlier, one of the characteristics of management in SMEs is the dominant role of the founder–owner–managers in this process. This fact is confirmed by research which shows, among other things, that their high level of education and their management experience increases their willingness to invest in human capital (Harney & Alkhalaf, 2020). This is because they are associated with a greater awareness of the importance of human capital as a factor of competitiveness for SMEs and the appreciation of the effectiveness of HRM. In combination with a management style based on building employee engagement and developing practices aimed at the effective acquisition, development, and retention of employees, such an approach to HR translates into the increased performance of SMEs. These issues determine the level of professionalisation of HRM in SMEs. The professionalisation of owner–managers is reflected in their competencies, including those related to HR as well as their values and social orientations. It can be assumed that their high level of awareness and values lead to the initiation and implementation of HR processes that are adequate in a given situation, the delegation of tasks and responsibilities to other people and to hiring specialists or establishing cooperation with external consultants in order to design, implement and improve HRM practices (Pocztowski & Pauli, 2013). The issue of the professionalisation of HRM in SMEs becomes particularly important in the context of the early internationalisation of SMEs. This is because new task areas for managers arise here that go beyond the scope of entrepreneurship and traditional HRM in SMEs. These issues are highlighted in the following sections.

Summarising the typical characteristics of HRM in the SMEs presented above, it is worth noting the dominant owner–manager perspective in the study of HRM practices and the shortcomings in including the perspective of the employees of these companies in the research (Harney & Alkhalaf, 2020). There is therefore a cognitive gap here, given the key role played by human capital in this type of company. It seems that paying more attention to employees' perception of HRM practices and changing the approach to studying HRM in SMEs as a predetermined and intended practice toward exploring it without preconceptions opens up new possibilities for a more in-depth understanding of the essence and specificity of HRM in SMEs. It is important to explore the issue of change management in SMEs in the context of applying new models of employment in the conditions of the so-called 'new normal' emerging after crises, such as the Covid-19 pandemic, or when deciding to enter the international market. Among the many questions to be answered are those concerning the relationship between the performance and the resilience of SMEs as well as to what extent HRM practices are changing, and what factors influence this process. How do disruptive technologies change the philosophy and practices of HRM? What contribution can HRM make to the creation of stakeholder value? How do owner–managers manage these changes? To what extent do these changes differ in micro-, small- and medium-sized enterprises? Investigating the above issues requires a more holistic and context-sensitive approach that takes into account the contributions of different research perspectives reported in the literature, namely universalistic (best practice), contingency (best fit or matching models), resource-based theories and ecological theories (Harney, 2021). This allows the use of different approaches to the role of HRM in SMEs and attempts to overcome the limitations of different research approaches, thus allowing better recognition of the specificity of HRM in these enterprises.

3.2 Limited transferability of HRM practices developed in the context of MNCs

As emphasised in the previous section, HRM in SMEs is highly context-specific and characterised by reactivity. The triggers may be different situations, which undoubtedly include early internationalisation. The question of the mechanism of introducing specific HRM practices in connection with the internationalisation process of SMEs and the possibility of using the experience of multinational corporations in this field is therefore relevant. The literature on international human resource management points to some characteristic features of HRM in companies operating in international markets. These include the increased scope and complexity of tasks, a greater diversity of human resources, a broader context for identifying and addressing HRM issues, greater interference in employees' personal lives, and the high importance of cross-cultural competencies, and increased personnel risk (Tarique et al., 2016; Dowling et al., 2008; Harzing & Pinnington, 2015).

Today, the scope of international human resource management includes three main research and implementation areas also referred to as trends or developmental trajectories, namely HRM in multinational enterprises, comparative HRM and cross-cultural management (Morley, 2007; Dowling et al., 2008). Within the trend of HRM in multinational enterprises, universal HRM policies and practices related to recruitment and selection, performance management, appraisal, reward and development are the subjects of research and implementation. There are also issues specific to HRM in the international context, such as the relationship between the head office and subsidiaries and branches of a multinational company located in foreign markets, expatriation and international assignments. Within the trend of Comparative International Human Resource Management, research is aimed at identifying and analysing similarities and differences in human resource management at national and regional levels and across industry sections (Brewster & Mayrhofer, 2012; Brewster et al., 2018). Comparative research covers an increasing number of countries, which is undoubtedly a result of globalisation and the associated foreign direct investment located in different countries and other regions of the world (Morley et al., 2009; Dickmann et al., 2016). The cross-cultural trend is characterised by the application of the cultural perspective to the study of HR issues and organisational behaviour in companies operating in an international context. The above trends of international HRM are intertwined and complementary, forming the basis for studying, understanding, and resolving various HR issues in the context of globalisation and other determinants of HRM policies and practices, not only in multinational corporations but also in SMEs operating in international markets. Knowledge of human resource management in companies operating across borders and its skilful application is a current issue for researchers and managers. Future research in this area should consider context, process, time and synergies between comparative HRM and HRM in MNCs (Brewster et al., 2017).

Taking into account the issues discussed in the previous chapters of this book related to the process of the internationalisation of SMEs, particularly the early internationalisation of SMEs and their specific features in general, it is reasonable to ask a question about the transferability of the results of research carried out within the different HRM trends and in different countries, industries and companies, as well as the transferability of HRM practices developed in transnational corporations to SMEs in the process of early internationalisation. At the outset, it should be noted that the already quoted publications indicate the limited possibility of such transferability due to the above-mentioned characteristics of SMEs, in which even if the basic HRM functions are similar to those in large enterprises, the way they are performed is different, often simplified and at a lower level from the point of view of professional HRM. However, it is worth asking the following question of whether the lower level of formalisation of HRM strategies, structures, and processes, or the absence of an HR department in SMEs, especially in small companies, implies a lower level of HRM in those companies. P. Sparrow points out that practices such as employee involvement schemas, teamwork, control systems and culture-change programmes can be found in SMEs (Sheehan, 2014). In turn, the direct influence of the owner–manager and group culture can be a substitute for certain HR practices (Harney & Alkhalaf, 2020). Thus, it can be assumed that the distinctiveness of HRM in SMEs does not automatically imply a lower level of management even when dealing with the specific HR problems that occur in the process of internationalisation. This issue requires further research in the context of the adaptability of universal HRM knowledge and practices developed in MNCs to the specificity of early internationalised SMEs.

At this point, it is worth noting that the internationalisation of business involves many challenges in the area of work and human resources. These include managing multinational teams, developing international management, finding culturally appropriate leadership styles, overcoming communication barriers through intercultural communication training, attracting and integrating employees from different cultures (including in the personnel-selection-process criteria that determine the ability to work abroad), and building remuneration systems that take into account international differences in salary levels, labour costs, productivity, working time, and social benefits.

The following issues are some of the areas in the field of international HRM that have been explored and described in the literature and can inspire and be used to improve the professionalism of HRM in early internationalised SMEs and determine appropriate HRM practices. These issues can be analysed in the context of the individual, organisational and contextual determinants of HRM practices.

A key issue in individual terms is the international orientation of managers, which determines, among other things, the HRM practices applied. In the case of SMEs, this is the orientation of owner–managers expressing their perception of international business and their approach to people management. To examine this orientation, the well-known Perlmutter typology can be used, which distinguishes four orientations: ethnocentric, regiocentric, polycentric, and geocentric (Perlmutter, 1969; Heenan & Perlmutter, 1979). On this basis, the strategies of early internationalised SMEs, their structural solutions, stakeholder cooperation models and HRM practices can be identified. The identification of the owner's–manager's dominant orientation towards international markets enables prediction of the approach to HRM and may be a starting point for investing in the development of their and other managers' competencies. Among the areas requiring development, the global mindset should be considered to be particularly important in the context of internationalisation. This includes cognitive, emotional and behavioural elements characterised by an openness to cultural differences and a readiness to act in a diverse international environment. The global mindset is a kind of meta-competence enabling one to see the world from a broader perspective and work effectively in a culturally diverse environment. In connection with such features as entrepreneurship and professional experience, the global mindset positively influences coping with global competition, managing change, communicating in a culturally diverse work environment, and leading teams in such conditions. The development of the global mindset in owner–managers, due to their special role in SMEs, is a factor supporting the spread of this mindset among other managers and employees, contributing to the development of the given company in the international market.

The organisational aspects of HRM in international companies include the organisational structure, the architecture of HR functions and HRM procedures. These are used to integrate HRM activities in different markets and coordinate policies and practices abroad with those of the head office. Specific solutions to organisational HR issues depend, among other factors, on the size of the company, the stage of its development, the time it has been active in foreign markets, the scope and complexity of its business operations, the management strategy determining the extent of standardisation and centralisation versus local fit and decentralisation needs, and technology and the state's involvement in business processes (Briscoe et al., 2009; Tarique et al., 2016).

It seems that SMEs can benefit from the rich experiences of large multinationals by appropriately adapting them to the specifics of a small- or medium-sized company. However, the implementation of HRM processes in these companies requires a different approach than in transnational corporations. In the case of small companies which start their activity in foreign markets by selling their goods and services or by setting up, e.g. sales offices abroad; the structural solution would probably be to report directly to the owner–manager from the head office in the country of origin. In the case of a medium-sized company, there may be a similar practice which, as the company grows, may take on more elaborate structural solutions in the form of networks linking business partners in different countries with the structures of the head office. In the latter case, a separate organisational unit dealing with HR issues may be expected. Important tasks in the area of HR include the acquisition of employees to perform tasks abroad, the development of intercultural competencies necessary for effective work in a diverse environment, and the development of a remuneration system for these employees. It should be assumed that one of the conditions for the success of SMEs in international markets is the preparation and retention of specialists, referred to as expatriates, who can be delegated to work abroad. This concerns both traditional forms of expatriation connected with travelling for shorter and longer stays as well as new, non-standard forms of expatriation such as rotational assignments or virtual assignments. Irrespective of the form of expatriation that can be found in SMEs, they should prepare an adequate procedure in this field, including preparing employees for cooperation abroad, supporting them during the implementation of tasks and at the stage of completing the international assignment. An external consultant can assist in finding an adequate organisational solution that builds on the existing knowledge in this area as well as in other issues related to HR in an international work environment.

In conclusion, it is important to note that the internationalisation of SMEs goes hand in hand with the internationalisation of their human resource management. This internationalisation can involve both the extension of the existing structural solution through the creation of a job position or a larger organisational unit as well as through the internationalisation of the HRM competencies of the owner–manager and the HRM managers of the company. Considering the aforementioned specificity of HRM in SMEs, it can be stated that the elements of the HR-function architecture of SMEs operating in international markets are the owner–manager and an external provider of IHRM services, implementing activities such as expatriation, cultural and language training, compensation and benefits. For medium-sized companies, the HR-function architecture may include in-house HRM managers/specialists. Team leaders and employees and other persons working for the company remain an important element of this architecture in all cases.

The importance of context in the management of SMEs and its components has already been tentatively discussed. Thus, we will limit ourselves here to highlighting the international aspects of this context in terms of the applicability of the existing knowledge on IHRM determinants to the SME situation. In general, it can be said that the international context of HRM is characterised by a greater number of factors that determine HRM policies and practices. Among these factors, there are political and economic systems in the host countries which determine the rules of doing business, including those relating to HRM, e.g. rules on the employment of workers, the design of employment relationships, requirements concerning the working environment, health and safety standards and taxation. Institutional factors in the form of regulations and standards relating to working conditions and labour relations are important in international activity. These are the product of the activities of international organisations such as the United Nations, the International Labour Organisation, the Organisation for Economic Cooperation and Development, and the European Union (Briscoe et al., 2009).

Particularly important among contextual factors in international business are the socio-cultural characteristics of the host countries and the degree to which they differ from the characteristics of the company's home country. Differences in traditions, values, beliefs or behavioural patterns found in different countries where a company conducts its business are important in shaping adequate HR practices related to recruitment and selection, performance management, compensation, training and labour relations (Tarique et al., 2016). The contextual factors mentioned above determine the functioning of all organisations operating in the international space, including SMEs. For the latter, they pose particular challenges due to their lesser experience in operating in the diverse contexts of different countries, less bargaining power in dealing with host government agencies, limited resources, and the means to manage operations in international markets (Dowling et al., 2008). How complex the context of HRM is in different countries and regions, and how different contextual factors influence HRM practices is evidenced by publications that are in international circulation (Brewster & Mayrhofer, 2012; Dickmann et al., 2016; Brewster et al., 2018) and those produced in indigenous languages that are limited in access for a wider audience.

The individual organisational and contextual factors that determine the HRM practices of multinational enterprises, as outlined above, give rise to the question of the adaptability of certain solutions in organisations ranging from large multinationals to small- and medium-sized companies that operate in international markets, including early internationalised firms. At this point, it is worth referring to the issue of the cross-border transfer of HRM practices by multinational enterprises. The complexity of such ventures stems from the fact that these practices are embedded in the diverse context of the host countries where the company's subsidiaries are located. Three underlying reasons have been identified in an attempt to explain the interest in the transfer of HR practices: market (seeking efficiency gains), cultural (influence of cultural factors), and political (empowerment of specific actors within the organisation) (Edwards, 2015). Each of these perspectives makes some contribution to understanding the nature and determinants of the transfer of HRM practices between different countries, but only an integrated approach that considers all three mechanisms enables the development of an effective mechanism for transferring these practices. It can also be used in small and medium enterprises in the process of adopting specific HRM practices used in large companies as well as transferring practices developed in the head office of a small- or medium-sized company to the host markets where business is conducted. At this point, it is also worth emphasising the need for a holistic approach to the adaptation of specific HRM practices in SMEs, which was highlighted earlier.

3.3 Challenges for HRM resulting from early and rapid internationalisation

We begin our discussion of the HRM-related challenges arising from early and rapid internationalisation by identifying the key factors influencing this process at its various stages.

In Section 2.3, we listed a wide spectrum of individual, organisational and environmental determinants of SME internationalisation recognised in IB literature, where the accelerated pattern is either considered jointly with the incremental pattern or is simply excluded (Table 2.1). In Table 2.2, we have also compiled various conceptual frameworks containing the drives of internationalisation that are specific for early internationalised firms (EIFs). None of the above-mentioned conceptualisations, however, explain how exactly the set of individual, organisational and environmental factors changes along with the company's further presence in the international market.

To outline the dynamics of early and rapid internationalisation, we may apply a basic analytical framework containing three stages, namely pre-entry, entry, and post-entry (Rastrollo-Horrillo & Martin-Armario, 2019, p. 455). In this vein, Rialp-Criado et al. (2010) developed a conceptual model of born global development through the following phases: pre-start-up/venture creation, pre-internationalisation, and post-internationalisation. They suggested that these phases pose distinctive challenges for strategy formation; this starts with responsiveness to rapidly changing environmental factors (e.g. new market conditions, radical change in technology) followed by intensification of international networking and organisational learning, and finally, achieving a global competitive positioning (Rialp-Criado et al., 2010, p. 120).

A notable exemplification of the aforementioned three-stage framework is an exploratory study in eight BGs by Gabrielsson et al. (2008). In particular, the researchers identified the following phases of development in these companies: (1) introduction, (2) growth and resource accumulation, and (3) break out. The first stage precedes entering the international market, when the enterprise has an underdeveloped organisational structure and limited human resources. Such a company heavily relies on a few individuals who possess 'unique skills combined with entrepreneurship [that] (…) lead to the development of unique products with global market potential' (Gabrielsson et al., 2008, p. 391). As the firm growth requires financing and international business experience, which is often insufficient at this stage, BGs tend to compensate for their own 'shortcomings' by collaborating with a few MNEs, developing channels/networking in the virtual space to create demand for their products, and also by recruiting managers/professionals with expertise in export or concerning specific foreign markets and who demonstrate a strong commitment to international operations (Gabrielsson & Kirpalani, 2004; Gabrielsson et al., 2008). In the second phase, BGs learn from their business partners and the channels and/or network members. The length of this period depends on the interaction between the industry's potential to become global and the firm's preparedness for globalisation. The latter reflects the ability of the BG to place its products on the global market and stems from organisational learning largely conditioned by the capability to acquire knowledge from its initial customers, both domestic and foreign (Gabrielsson et al., 2008, p. 396). In the final stage, BGs develop and implement a strategy that leverages on their organisational learning effort and the experience previously accumulated from global customers. This strategy allows them to break out of the initial network and independently seek new opportunities to expand globally. However, their further activity requires a global vision, effective commitment, and also additional resources. The sources of the latter include unique products that 'can result in self-generation of capital, (…) a public offering of shares to raise capital', and benefits from 'mergers and acquisitions or joint ventures or licensing of its product/service' (Gabrielsson et al., 2008, p. 397). At this stage, the BG eventually evolves to the 'normal' MNE.

The alternative conceptualisations of early and rapid internationalisation either reduce the number of stages (e.g. 'internationalising' and 'being internationalised' in a single-case study by Turcan and Juho, 2014), or increase it up to four. The latter approach was adopted, inter alia, by Gabrielsson and Gabrielsson (2013). Based on multiple case studies in high-tech B2B Finnish-based INVs, they recognised four stages in their international development, which included '(1) INV creation, (2) commercialisation and foreign entries, (3) rapid growth and foreign expansion, and (4) rationalisation and foreign maturity' (p. 1362). A similar framework was applied by Ciszewska-Mlinarič et al. (2020) in a single-case study in the CEE context.[1] The considered phases varied in terms of the dominant mode of learning (Ciszewska-Mlinarič et al., 2020) and the nature of management and foreign business problems (Gabrielsson & Gabrielsson, 2013), yet they all share the potential threat of a survival crisis that forces the INV to return to the previous phase or, at worst, leads to bankruptcy. Gabrielsson and Gabrielsson (2013, p. 1363) propose that overcoming the survival crises and solving the problems occurring in this process depends on firm-level factors, i.e. the knowledge of opportunities, learning, resources, capabilities and entrepreneurial orientation. However, the relative importance of these factors varies over time. In particular, opportunity creation, explorative learning and technology capabilities seem most important in the early phases, but in the subsequent stages, opportunity discovery, exploitative learning, marketing, and networking capabilities become more relevant

(Gabrielsson & Gabrielsson, 2013 p. 1370). This shift also applies to entrepreneurial orientation, which is the 'engine' of initial growth, but the excess of this feature may later even threaten the survival of INV (Gabrielsson & Gabrielsson, 2013; Gabrielsson et al., 2014).

Recent studies conducted on Italian manufacturing BGs have revealed a slightly different four-step pattern of international expansion (Romanello & Chiarvesio, 2017). In addition to pre-entry, entry, and post-entry stages, researchers identified a transitional period prior to the last phase. The peculiarity of this 'turning point', which typically occurs four to five years after setting up a company, consists of managing the transformation of individual capabilities into an organisational knowledge base, which is a challenging task for entrepreneurs and an important condition for the sustainable growth of the BG (p. 177). This implies a greater reliance on export managers and other collaborators due to the high complexity faced by the company, the emphasis on sharing knowledge at the inter-organisational level, and the involvement of founders in building commitment to the product, the brand and the company itself, and fulfilling the leading roles of coordinators and supervisors (p. 201).

Based on a few available studies focused on the process of early and rapid internationalisation (i.e. Gabrielsson & Gabrielsson, 2013; Almor et al., 2014; Gabrielsson et al., 2014; Hagen & Zucchella, 2014; Rastrollo-Horrillo & Martin-Armario, 2019; Ciszewska-Mlinarič et al., 2020), and also on literature reviews concerning the EIFs (e.g. Rialp et al., 2005; Romanello & Chiarvesio, 2019; Tuomisalo & Leppaaho, 2019) we may conclude that the relative importance of individual factors (related to founders/decision makers), both organisational and environmental, varies in particular phases. In the course of their development, BGs/INVs have to deal with several liabilities that affect their survival. More specifically, they experience the liability of foreignness relating to their foreign local competitors, the liability of newness concerning the competition with firms that operate in target markets for much longer periods, and finally their ability to cope with constraints stemming from their small size (Mudambi & Zahra, 2007; Prashantham & Young, 2011; Clark et al., 2018; Rastrollo-Horrillo & Martin-Armario, 2019). Along with accelerated internationalisation, the company's needs in terms of knowledge (Schwens & Kabst, 2009) and capabilities (Prange & Verdier, 2011) that foster the growth of EIFs rapidly change, and consequently different development stages require different learning modes and sources of this knowledge (Gabrielsson et al., 2008; Gabrielsson & Gabrielsson, 2013). Some authors even suggest a shift from the primacy of founders' prior experience and learning 'from the outside' in the early stages towards a greater emphasis on organisational knowledge and capabilities and learning 'from the inside' in the post-entry internationalisation phase (Rastrollo-Horrillo & Martin-Armario, 2019). Nevertheless, the empirical findings on learning processes and modes in the consecutive phases of accelerated internationalisation are fragmented and inconclusive, thus this issue requires further studies (Tuomisalo & Leppaaho 2019, p. 467).

Regarding the phases of early and rapid international expansion, it should be emphasised that post-entry internationalisation and reaching maturity by the EIFs are comparatively less studied (Rialp et al., 2005; Jones et al., 2011; Romanello & Chiarvesio, 2019; Ciszewska-Mlinarič et al., 2020). This stage of the company's development is all the more difficult to understand as it may be discontinuous (e.g. Nummela et al., 2022), and the changes do not have to be of an upward nature, e.g. the BG/INV may reduce its international commitment or even withdraw from a specific location/domain of activity (Vissak et al., 2020). Possible scenarios include: the failure or loss of independence by such a company (Sleuwaegen & Onkelinx, 2014); a slowdown in the growth rate and becoming similar to slow internationalisers/typical MNEs (Gabrielsson et al., 2008; Gabrielsson & Gabrielsson, 2013; Ciszewska -Mlinarič et al., 2020); growth through geographic diversification or increasing the intensity of foreign operations in existing markets (Almor & Hashai, 2004; Johanson & Martín Martín, 2015); maintaining a high growth rate through mergers and acquisitions (Almor et al., 2014), strategic partnerships, and entering complex markets that boosts knowledge base, enhance opportunities, and trigger innovation (Hagen & Zucchella, 2014). Such a variety in the behavioural patterns of EIFs in the post-entry stage, along with limited and inconsistent empirical knowledge on organisation-level drivers constitute a major source of challenges for HRM research and practice.

The extant research on BGs/INVs offers a rather limited insight into the role of HRM in the process of internationalisation. The empirical studies are particularly sparse, although some HRM-related issues appear in the conceptual works (Table 2.2 in Section 2.4). As far as the initial stages are concerned, these publications share the assumption that some individual human resources play a pivotal role here. This especially applies to the properties and background of founders or executives, including socio-cognitive and motivation-related components (e.g. global mindset, entrepreneurial orientation, leadership skills, strong motivation to expand internationally), prior international experience and personal networks. Considered jointly as a source of human capital at the individual level, they have been acknowledged as main drivers of accelerated internationalisation (Madsen & Servais, 1997; Nummela et al., 2004, Nummela et al., 2005; Kuivalainen et al., 2007; 2012; Romanello & Chiarvesio, 2019). They were also conceptualised as a primary factor affecting organisational resources and capabilities contributing to this process (Rialp et al., 2005; Weerawardena et al., 2007). The appreciation of the above attributes in the context of accelerated internationalisation involves a careful composition of the top management team (TMT) that ensures the appropriate configuration of knowledge, experience and networks provided by its members and the ability of such a team to expand the business internationally under the condition of limited human, physical, and financial resources.

Creating a TMT endowed with the required attributes can be considered as the major challenge for managing human resources in the initial phase of early and rapid internationalisation for several reasons. Firstly, the chances of attracting and selecting TMT members are limited due to the low availability of such people and the nature of the activities undertaken for this purpose, i.e. building a team through informal networks by an employer with limited own resources, who is unrecognisable to potential job candidates (Leung, 2003). Secondly, the need to differentiate this team in terms of resources and background and the urge to make quick decisions under conditions of uncertainty, ambiguity and volatility can be difficult to reconcile, especially when managerial skills and inclusive leadership are insufficient (Xing et al., 2020; Breuillot, 2021). Lastly, the dynamics of accelerated internationalisation requires an exceptional 'openness' from TMT members (Hagen & Zucchella, 2014) as well as learning new roles and unlearning old roles at a much faster pace compared to the incremental international expansion (Romanello & Chiarvesio, 2017). The latter requirement particularly applies to the aforementioned 'turning point' that precedes the post-entry stage.

With regard to the HRM practices in the post-entry phase of early and rapid internationalisation, the existent literature provides limited and fragmented evidence (Table 3.1), which leaves ample room for further research. This knowledge gap persists for various reasons, including the very limited number of empirical studies; research localisation restricted to only some Western European countries (Germany, Spain, France); limited generalisability of findings (prevalence of qualitative data, explorative case studies); a fairly narrow scope of the analysed issues, dominated by issues of staffing, sometimes supplemented with the use of training or work arrangements.

Table 3.1 HRM practices used by EIFs in post-entry internationalisation – A summary of previous empirical studies

Source	Materials and methods	HRM aspects/problems	Key findings on HRM-related issues
Isidor et al. (2011)	Primary quantitative data from survey in 116 German-based medium-sized enterprises possessing foreign subsidiaries/affiliates/joint ventures, including early and late internationalisers EIFs defined as companies that became active on an international level within the first five years from their foundation Regression analyses	International orientation in staffing policies (according to Perlmutter's EPRG taxonomy) performed by EIFs compared with late internationalisers Selected determinants of international staffing in EIFs: 1 Degree of prior international experience of managerial teams 2 Technological intensity of their products 3 The amount of network contacts in the foreign market	1 Contrary to expectations, prior international experience of TMT is not at all associated with the firms' international staffing. 2 Technological intensity increases the probability of the choice of an ethnocentric staffing policy, especially for EIFs. 3 Networks enable EIFs to pursue regiocentric or geocentric staffing policies, but they do not have any significant impact on late internationalisers.
Glaister et al. (2014)	Secondary quantitative data from the World Bank's enterprise survey project conducted between 2006 and 2010 Sample of 890 firms in 29 countries (emerging economies) that started exporting within three years from their foundation Regression analyses	Employment of temporary and skilled employees and the provision of training in mature BGs The impact of employment size as an independent variable Other organisational factors included as control variables: age of the firm, extent of foreign investment, export intensity	1 With the increase in size, the BGs shift from the externalised, market-based approaches (i.e. based on temporary workers) to more internalised, commitment-based approaches (i.e. based on skilled employees and greater usage of training). 2 The level of temporary employment increases with age, export intensity and foreign investment. 3 The use of skilled employees is higher in more export-dependent BGs.

(Continued)

Table 3.1 (Continued)

Source	Materials and methods	HRM aspects/problems	Key findings on HRM-related issues
Ripollé et al. (2018)	Primary qualitative data from six Spanish-based BGs operating in various industries Explorative multiple case study	Recruitment, training and employee engagement in expanding the knowledge base of BGs	Common features of investigated BGs: 1 They demonstrate a strong interest in having stable and well-trained employees and a high proportion of permanent employees (exceeding 70%). 2 They prefer young workers with foreign language fluency 3 They compensate a limited possibility to attract candidates by means of high salary by ensuring job security, autonomy, and flexible work arrangements. 4 Indirect forms of employee participation are not used in these firms 5 Knowledge sharing is supported by the design of the workspace, a use of teams, the availability of technical means of communication, favourable working atmosphere and regular meetings 6 They adopt a formalised, systematic and standardised recruitment and induction procedure developed and refined by entrepreneurs in the early years of operating through learning from experience; 7 They use different external tools to identify and attract candidates with an emphasis on networks developed by entrepreneurs

including incubators, universities and vocation schools (networks as 'staff provider');

8 The selection process is based on face-to-face interviews focused on education profile rather than on prior work experience (except for managerial jobs).

9 They offer limited formal training and strongly opt for on-the-job training and internships, and encourage employees to take part in external specific/technical education programmes.

Study	Data/Methodology	HRM practices	Key findings
Hernández (2019)	Primary qualitative data from several high-tech Spanish-based INVs, defined as companies that started receiving foreign revenues within the first three years of starting productive activity and aged from three to seven years Explorative multiple case study	HRM practices that foster employee entrepreneurial behaviour (EEB) in high-tech INVs – the scope of these practices include 1 Opportunity enhancing employee participation, communication, flat organisational structure, socialisation, autonomy, flexibility and person-job fit 2 Ability enhancing recruitment and training 3 Motivation enhancing incentives	1 HRM practices aimed at enhancing opportunity seem to be most relevant for achieving EEB. 2 A common characteristic of HRM practices implemented in the investigated companies is that 'the entrepreneur intends to engage the employees in the whole organizational project' (p. 19).

(*Continued*)

Table 3.1 (Continued)

Source	Materials and methods	HRM aspects/problems	Key findings on HRM-related issues
Breuillot (2021)	Primary qualitative data from eight French-based EIFs, defined as companies that started international activity through any entry mode within three years of their foundation Sample included young and more established ventures, operating from 2.5 to 19 years Explorative multiple case study	Influence of human resource diversity and diversity management on internationalisation process in EIFs Dimensions of HR diversity: cultural or national origin, gender, experience, knowledge). HRM practices considered from DM: recruitment, communication, team-building, work design, employee autonomy, use of training	Three patterns of DM in EIFs were revealed: resistance, access and legitimacy, and learning. Based on the findings, the following propositions were developed (pp. 143–145): 1 If EIFs implement a learning perspective on DM, HR diversity becomes a strategic resource for the internationalisation process, in the case of an access and legitimacy perspective, it becomes an ordinary resource, while from the resistance perspective, its role is negative. 2 DM is a determinant of progress in the internationalisation of EIFs and reaching a post-entry phase, which is conditional on the implementation of a learning perspective prior to the transition phase and preferably from its inception. 3 To leverage the benefits from the learning perspective for progress in the internationalisation of EIFs, these firms must proactively implement both diversity- programme practices and general management practices.

Source: own elaboration based on literature.

Based on the empirical studies presented in Table 3.1, several conclusions can be drawn. Firstly, in mature EIFs, the recruitment policy increases the emphasis on creating an internal knowledge base by hiring qualified job candidates or young 'potentials' with foreign language fluency, which does not, however, mean resignation from temporary workers. Secondly, the entrepreneur's networks still play a key role in staffing policy. Thirdly, the level of formal training is indeed low, but other practices are used to support knowledge sharing and learning in the workplace, and to encourage entrepreneurial behaviour, including those related to work organisation/design, communication, direct participation and employee autonomy (Glaister et al., 2014; Ripollé et al., 2018; Hernandez, 2019). Next, some companies have implemented solutions promoting HR diversity in the areas of recruitment, work organisation and training, but the actual strategic contribution of such diversity is conditioned by the integration of DM and general managing practices (Breuillot, 2021). Finally, HRM practices are context-independent, as shown by the differences between EIFs due to the level of their technological intensity (Isidor et al., 2011; Hernandez, 2019), export intensity (Glaister et al., 2014) and the institutional environment in which they are located (Ripollé et al., 2018).

The above findings provide us with a preliminary diagnosis, which undoubtedly requires further verification and enrichment with empirical knowledge on HR processes and other important issues such as the strategic importance of HRM, the professionalisation and formalisation of HRM practices and various HRM-related problems specific to SME internationalisation discussed in the previous parts of this book. The questions that we are seeking answers to in our empirical research therefore constitute another step in reducing this gap.

Note

1 The scope of analysis covered the period from 1992 to 2017, i.e. from the foundation of an international new venture until it became a large MNE. The development of this company was split into (1) pre-internationalisation, 1992–1994; (2) early internationalisation, 1995–1998; (3) adolescent internationalisation, 1997–2007; (4) mature internationalisation, 2008–2017 (Ciszewska-Mlinarič et al., 2020, pp. 454–460).

4 Methodological aspects of empirical study

4.1 Theoretical background and conceptual framework

Drawing on the literature studies discussed in previous chapters, we identified the gap in the extant knowledge relating to HRM in SMEs operating internationally. In particular, the dearth of empirical research in this field concerns the early and rapid internationalisation after entering foreign markets. Undoubtedly, findings from the few prior empirical works (Subchapter 3.3) do not provide a sufficient basis to answer the question of the role that HRM plays in more advanced phases of accelerated internationalisation, which is why our research is of an exploratory nature. Consequently, to examine this issue more comprehensively, we have adopted a mixed approach, consisting of quantitative and qualitative analysis of data collected from the survey and in-depth interviews. To specify the research problem, we developed the following questions:

RQ1 *How important is HRM for EIFs after their entry to foreign markets?*

RQ2 *What configurations of HRM practices are used by EIFs with regard to their various trajectories of post-entry internationalisation?*

RQ3 *Do they differ from practices adopted by their late internationalised counter-partners?*

RQ4 *In what way do the HRM practices respond to the challenges faced by EIFs at this stage?*

RQ5 *What are the outcomes of these practices in early internationalised SMEs?*

DOI: 10.4324/9781003319979-4

As previously mentioned, the research design consisted of both quantitative and qualitative studies. The former were aimed at exploring the relevance of HRM in EIFs (RQ1), identifying the configurations of HRM practices used by EIFs that follow different trajectories in the post-entry phase (RQ2), and comparing them with late internationalised SMEs (RQ3). The qualitative research was intended to complement and verify the findings of the first stage (regarding RQ1, RQ2) and deepen the diagnosis of HRM practices in respect of the specific challenges faced by EIFs at this stage of internationalisation (RQ4) and the outcomes of these practices (RQ5). The choice of research questions defining the scope of the research results from the premises presented below.

The internationalisation of SMEs differs from the experience of large companies in numerous ways, including their greater sensitivity to the external environment and flexible modus operandi 'enforced' by limited resources and external contingencies (Subchapter 2.3). However, those SMEs that follow early and rapid patterns of internationalisation (Subchapters 2.4 and 3.3) learn differently from late internationals – they also face the challenges involved in the 'turning point' in their further development. At this stage, further expansion requires transforming the individual knowledge of the founders into organisational resources and competences as the development of the organisational knowledge base helps EIFs to survive and succeed in the long term. This is all the more difficult due to the variety of post-entry internationalisation trajectories followed by the EIFs identified in previous studies, which in turn may translate into different needs in terms of resources and organisational capabilities. To sum up, we make the following assumptions: firstly, in the later stages of internationalisation, HRM practices may have a greater contribution to the success of EIFs; secondly, the specificity of the experience of EIFs from accelerated internationalisation may result in different HRM practices (compared to late internationalised SMEs); thirdly, the variety of scenarios in post-entry development can be an important source of variation in these practices amongst EIFs; lastly, external contingencies remain especially important for HRM in those EIFs which continue to operate as internationalised SMEs in the later stages of their life.

Regardless of the consequences of early and rapid internationalisation, the analysed organisations retain at least some of the characteristics of SMEs (discussed in Chapter 2). These features determine which HR-related activities are undertaken and in what way (Subchapter 3.1). They also limit the possibilities of transferring HRM practices implemented in large MNEs (Subchapter 3.2). For the above reasons, the diagnosis of HRM practices used in EIFs also requires taking into account the characteristics of the organisation that are not directly related to internationalisation but still apply to SMEs.

In our study we adopt the resource-based perspective, but we also draw from the BG/INV theory due to the specificity of the investigated organisations, from the configurational approach in relation to HRM practices as well as from the contingency theory due to the impact of various contextual factors, which excludes the possibility of indicating a universal (best) solution. More specifically, we assume that EIFs can compete successfully in international markets and continue their expansion owing to their organisational capabilities with regard to integrating and deploying valuable, rare, inimitable, and non-substitutable resources (Wernerfelt, 1984; Grant, 1991), which in the case of HR, relates to the capability to manage human resources. This especially applies to more advanced phases of internationalisation, where the existent literature on BGs/INVs suggests the more prominent role of human resources at the organisational level. In line with the configurational approach, our analysis is focused on various sets of HRM practices. The core idea of this approach is that HRM practices 'cannot be implemented effectively in isolation, and that it is the combination of practices into a coherent package that matters' (Marchington & Grugulis, 2000, p. 1112). Drawing from the contingency perspective (Donaldson, 2001, p. 2), we claim that various bundles of HRM practices can produce successful HR-related, organisational, or business outcomes, depending on their fit to external and internal contextual factors.

For analysis of the qualitative data, we have developed a conceptual framework (Figure 4.1) to organise the empirical material and to

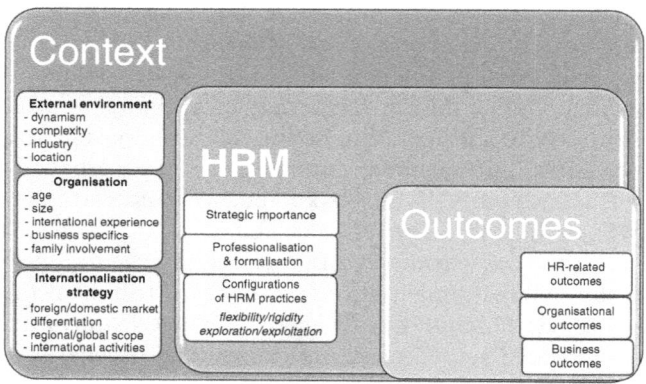

Figure 4.1 The conceptual framework of HRM in EIFs at the post-entry stage of internationalisation.

structure the discussion of findings, which consist of three core components: HRM, its outcomes, and context. Based on our findings from the literature study, we propose three main categories of factors that define the context of HRM practices in EIFs. These are as follows:

•   **Characteristics of the external environment** including environmental dynamism, international complexity, industry, and location specificity. As it was impossible to encompass all potentially important sources of external tensions influencing SMEs (discussed in Subchapter 2.2), the scope of our study was narrowed to those features that were found particularly important in prior research concerning EIFs and HRM in internationalised SMEs. Thus, we focus on environmental dynamism and complexity recognised as the most challenging aspects for HRM practices in SMEs operating internationally, including the acquiring/improvement of specific competencies possessed by core employees, developing leaders, hiring temporary workers and highly qualified permanent employees, HRM formalisation, and the usage of training programmes (Hsu et al., 2013; Glaister et al., 2014; Psychogios et al., 2016; Cortellazzo et al., 2020). **Complexity** refers to a situation 'characterised by many interconnected parts' resulting from the multitude of foreign markets and their geographic dispersion (Bennett & Lemoine, 2014, p. 313). In the case of internationalised SMEs, this complexity 'arises from the diversity among cultures, customers, competitors, and regulations' (Hsu et al., 2013, p. 2). **Environmental dynamism** can be defined as 'the rate and the instability of environmental change' resulting in the 'increased inability to assess accurately both the present and future state of the environment' of entrepreneurs/managers (Simerly & Li, 2002, p. 38). In HRM literature, this notion is interpreted in terms of the 'managerial perception of environmental uncertainties' emanating from changes in technology, composition of the customer base, preferences of customers, and market competition (Ketkar & Sett, 2010, p. 1178), which impede the anticipation of specific tasks performed by employees (Lepak et al., 2003, p. 686), and thus require greater flexibility in employees' properties and HRM practices (Ketkar & Sett, 2010; Hansen et al., 2019). As for the **industry**, prior studies on HRM in BGs/INVs suggest that some HRM practices (e.g. the use of training, hiring temporary workers and qualified job candidates) vary across industries (Glaister et al., 2014). Moreover, operating in high-tech industries can have an impact upon staffing policies (Isidor et al., 2011), and the usage of opportunity-enhancing practices, such as employee participation, autonomy, and flexibility in work design as well as a greater appreciation of person-job fit (Hernández, 2019). Furthermore, we may assume that operating in high-tech industries involves a greater emphasis on the specific technical competencies of job candidates and employees. In addition to the above features, we include the **location specificity** (discussed in Subchapter 5.1), which is in line with the comparative studies on HRM practices demonstrating differences across countries and regions (Morley et al., 2016; Berber et al., 2017; Cranet, 2017). It should be noted, however, that Poland as the home country is not a source of differentiation in HRM practices but rather a 'common denominator' for the investigated companies.

• **Characteristics of the organisation** that reflects its actual resources and capabilities resulting from (1) the period of business activity (i.e. age of the firm), which is important when facing the liability of newness; (2) the available labour resources defined by the employment size, which is relevant in case of the liability of smallness; (3) the acquired and accumulated international experience at firm-level, which is necessary to overcome the liability of foreignness (Mudambi & Zahra, 2007; Prashantham & Young, 2011; Clark et al., 2018; Rastrollo-Horrillo & Martin-Armario, 2019). In addition, we included the organisational features identified in prior studies as relevant determinants of HRM practices utilised by internationalised SMEs, including EIFs, namely the specificity of the business (e.g. profile of firm activity, type of products, and customers; Isidor et al., 2011; Glaister et al., 2014; Psychogios et al., 2016; Ripollé et al., 2018) as well as the possible involvement of the founder's family (i.e. family/non-family businesses; Bannò & Sgobbi, 2016; D'Angelo et al., 2016; Majocchi et al., 2018).

• **Internationalisation strategy** that positions the **foreign markets in relation to the domestic** one (i.e. the extent of internationalisation) and defines the **differentiation** of these markets and their **scope** (regional or global path) and **forms of international activities** (all discussed in Subchapter 2.2). This strategy results from the way in which foreign markets are perceived by key decision-makers (entrepreneurial/top management team), their attitudes towards internationalisation (Nummela et al., 2004; Baum et al., 2014; Lazaris & Freeman, 2018) and their aspirations and competencies related to running business on an international scale (Madsen & Servais, 1997; Gruenhagen et al., 2018; Cortelazzo et al., 2020) as well as networking skills (Freeman et al., 2006; Manolova et al., 2010; Freeman, 2014).

It should be emphasised that in reality, the above factors do not affect HRM in an isolated way. Therefore, we assume that various combinations of these factors pose specific challenges for HRM, considered in terms of the strategic importance of personnel function, professionalisation and formalisation, and bundles of HRM practices applied in EIFs. Direct evidence of the **strategic importance** of the personnel function is a strategy that defines future priorities and key activities in this field, consistent with the business strategy. Importantly, the presence of such a strategy reflects the professionalisation of HRM (Pocztowski et al., 2021). In a broader sense, **professionalisation** in this area also manifests in the development of HR competencies held by key decision-makers (entrepreneurial/top management team), cooperation with external entities possessing expertise in the HR area, and/or developing in-house HR professionals (along with the increase in employment size) that all together contribute to the professionalisation of HRM practices. **Formalisation**, regarded by some authors as a manifestation of professionalisation (Madison et al., 2018, p. 325), involves using a set of written procedures and rules to develop comprehensive HR structures to attract and deploy appropriate job candidates, develop in-house competencies, and motivate and retain valuable employees (Sánchez-Marín et al., 2019, p. 1087). The range of **HRM practices** under consideration includes work structuring, recruitment and selection, training and development, employee appraisal and remuneration, and performance management. The concept of **configurations** is adopted from Lepak and Snell (1999, 2002). These authors claim that organisations utilise various modes of employment resulting in different categories of human capital (HC), and thus they need to apply different bundles of HRM practices corresponding with these HC categories in order to achieve their goals (Lepak & Snell, 1999, 2002). In accordance with these objectives, there are four configurations of these practices:

- commitment-based HRM for highly unique and strategically valuable HC (residing in knowledge-based employees) that focuses on competence development within the organisation and nurturing long-term employee commitment;
- collaboration-based HRM for highly unique HC of low strategic value (derived from alliances and partnerships) that puts emphasis on establishing and maintaining interpersonal relationships, which serve as a pipeline to provide the company with the flow of valuable knowledge and unique skills;
- productivity-based HRM for strategically valuable HC with a low firm-specificity (obtained from job-based employment) whose

main concern is ensuring a good person-job fit by recruiting employees with competencies/properties needed to perform clearly defined jobs and capable of achieving the expected outcomes;

- compliance-based HRM for HC of low level in both dimensions (provided by contract workers) that emphasises compliance with precisely defined standards, requirements, and contractual arrangements and enables the company to improve cost-effectiveness.

These configurations of HRM practices can and should be combined in various architectures that enable the organisation to keep pace with different dynamic environments by addressing its need for flexibility (Hansen et al., 2019, p. 651). More specifically, greater **flexibility** in HR resources is ensured by architectures built around the commitment-based configuration, while the compliance-based configuration supports flexibility in terms of employment size (Lepak et al., 2003; Ketkar & Sett, 2010). By contrast, architectures dominated by the productivity-based approach tend to be more **rigid**, as it addresses full-time permanent employees specialised in performing well-defined, preprogrammed, repetitive tasks, which makes their adaptation to change much more challenging (Lepak et al., 2003, p. 685). Consistent with the above, some authors consider the aforementioned 'combinations' as means of balancing exploitative and exploratory learning at the firm level (Medcof & Song, 2013; Hansen et al., 2019), where **exploitation** involves the incremental refinement of existing knowledge in pursuit of high efficiency and **exploration** reflects adaptive behaviour focused on new knowledge, which implies search and experimentation (Lavie et al., 2010). According to Hansen et al. (2019), the core of explorative HR architecture is a commitment-based model, and the exploitative design is based on the compliance-based set of practices, while other bundles of practices might complement the above architectures differently, depending on environmental contingencies. As Lavie et al. (2010) posit, such an exploration-exploitation 'compromise' should reflect the strategic intentions of the management related to the company's development (which is incorporated in the strategic component of our conceptual framework); however, the relative importance of these two modes also depends on environmental factors, the current state of the company's resources and capabilities, its size, maturity, and experience (which are included in external and organisational characteristics, respectively).

The final component of our framework is the **outcomes of HRM**. Following Pocztowski et al. (2021), we distinguished three categories of these outcomes, namely HR-related, organisational, and business. Due to the specific context of this study, we focused, however, on the outcomes related to international expansion, such as ensuring that employees are qualified for working in an internationalised company and responding to other employee-related issues arising from internationalisation (**HR-related outcomes**); innovations (substantial improvements) in products, services, and processes (**organisational outcomes**); changes in sales growth, including foreign sales, profitability, market share, cost optimisation, and resilience in coping with the pandemic crisis (**business outcomes**).

4.2 Research instruments in quantitative and qualitative studies

Based upon a previous literature review, we developed two research instruments – a structured questionnaire used in the survey and a semi-structured questionnaire to conduct in-depth interviews. Both tools were built around the variables concerning HRM, contextual factors and outcomes. Nevertheless, only qualitative study provides full coverage of the constructs outlined in the conceptual framework (Figure 4.1). This 'inconsistency' arises from different sets of research problems addressed by the quantitative and qualitative steps of the project and the constraints related to the nature of the survey questionnaire (number and type of questions that can be applied).

The survey questionnaire consisted of thirty questions, where four questions concerned HRM practices and one related to innovation contained from several items.[1] The questions were organised into the following six blocks: (1) characteristics of the company and its international activity; (2) employment; (3) HRM practices; (4) innovation and business performance; (5) the impact of the Covid-19 pandemic; (6) characteristics of the respondent. The scope of the quantitative study included the following variables:

1   the characteristics of the external environment such as the industry and the international complexity;
2   the characteristics of organisation comprising the size, age, international experience, profile of activity, and the family/non-family nature of the business;
3   the international strategy encompassing the extent and the scope of internationalisation as well as the forms of participation in foreign markets;
4   HRM considered in terms of the strategy in this field and the configurations of HRM practices adopted by investigated firms;
5   outcomes limited to firm innovation and sales growth.

At the outset, it is worth emphasising that whenever it was possible, we adopted measures that were used in previous empirical studies. Thus, the industry specifics, which in our study refers to the distinction between high-tech and other sectors, were adopted from Piva et al. (2013). As we define international complexity as a result of operating in numerous and dispersed locations, we measured this aspect both with regard to the number of foreign markets and the number of geographical regions in which the firm's activities are dispersed. In the second case, we followed previous research on geographic diversification (Patel et al., 2018; Freixanet & Renart, 2020) that distinguished eight export areas: South and Central America, North America, the Far East and Central Asia, Sub-Saharan Africa, Maghreb (Morocco, Algeria, Tunisia, and Libya), Oceania, the European Union, and other European Countries.

In line with other studies (e.g. Bannó & Sgobbi, 2016; Hennart et al., 2019; Sánchez-Marín et al., 2019), we operationalised the size as the total number of employees and the age as the number of years from the foundation of the firm to the present (i.e. from 2021 to when the survey was first conducted). International experience of the company, defined in Subchapter 2.3 as a cumulative result of its presence in foreign markets, is measured as the number of years since it started exporting on a consistent basis (Contractor et al., 2005). With regard to the profile of activity, we split it into binary variables for manufacturing and services. Following Madison et al. (2018, p. 330), we distinguished between family and non-family businesses by asking whether the founder's family members remain the major owner(s) of the firm and at least two family members are working there.

The extent of international expansion, also defined as export intensity, scale, or degree of internationalisation (Subchapter 2.3), was measured as the foreign-sales-to-total-sales ratio (FSTS; e.g. Cesinger et al., 2012; Kuivalainen et al., 2012; Øyna & Alon, 2018). In line with Lopez et al. (2009), D'Angelo et al. (2013) and Baum et al. (2015) we operationalised the scope in terms of regional (i.e. operations within Europe) and global (i.e. including operations beyond European countries) patterns of internationalisation. Regarding forms of international activity, all investigated companies use exporting, thus the only measure of this variable applies to equity modes. In particular, we followed Chi et al. (2003), who developed a binary variable reflecting the answers to the question 'Does your company have foreign direct investments (i.e. it holds at least 10% of shares or stocks of the entities located broad)?' Similarly, we pose the question 'Does your company have an HR (or human resource management) strategy?' to measure the strategic importance of the personnel function on the basis of respondents' answers. Positive responses were coded as '1', while negative responses were coded as '0', and the same method was utilised for all categorical variables, including the HT/non-HT industry, family/non-family status, the profile of activity, and the scope and forms of international activity.

To measure the use of four configurations of HRM practices (commitment, collaboration, compliance, and productivity-based HRM), we adopted questionnaire items from Lepak and Snell (2002). Following their approach, we operationalised them as the additive indices of HRM practices and calculated each index by taking the mean value of the items belonging to the given configuration (Lepak & Snell, 2002, p. 526). However, instead of the original five-point Likert scale, we applied a seven-point scale because the latter might better address the dilemma of forced choosing between two equally undesirable points and thus provide a more accurate measure of a respondent's true evaluation (Finstad, 2010). Importantly, the original set of these items has been slightly modified. Due to the specificity of Polish SMEs, including customary rewarding practices, we replaced the statement concerning the employee stock ownership programs with the following phrase: 'long-term financial incentives/benefits/programs for employees'. In addition, one item was dropped ('compensation/rewards ... are designed to ensure equity with peers') due to its ambiguity signalled by the participants of this study. Finally, as the respondents were Poles, it was necessary to adapt the original items to the context of the study through the back translation procedure (Brislin, 1970) that ensures their linguistic equivalence. To grasp the essence of the HRM approach in the examined firms, we instructed the participants of the study to assess practices used continuously in their organisations over a three-year period (2018–2020). The creation of indices for individual configurations was preceded by an analysis of the reliability of the scales. For commitment-based, collaboration-based, and productivity-based HRM, standardised Cronbach's alpha coefficients (CA) were above the acceptable level, reaching 0.871, 0.812, and 0.806, respectively. However, the original set of items for the compliance-based configuration did not meet this requirement (the initial CA value was 0.422). We achieved an acceptable CA level of 0.663 by reducing this set to three items: (1) in my firm, the employees perform jobs that are well defined; (2) our training activities for the employees focus on compliance with rules, regulations, and procedures; (3) performance appraisals for the employees assess the compliance with present behaviours, procedures, and standards.

The average sales growth served as a measure of business outcome which is in line with findings by Rauch and Hatak (2016) on the most frequently used operationalisation in the SME context. However, as participants of the study appeared incapable or unwilling to provide accurate data, which might have lowered the rate of return, an ordinal measure was introduced instead. With regard to firm innovation, we adopted a three-item seven-point Likert scale from Zhou et al. (2013), in which the respondents assessed the extent to which their company had exploited new advanced technologies, developed new products or services, and adopted new approaches concerning logistics, distribution, or internal organisational processes in the previous three years. The standardised value of CA for this scale achieved an acceptable level of 0.793. Finally, to include the possible impact of the Covid-19 pandemic on HRM, we asked respondents whether the pandemic substantially affected the employment, wages, and training expenses (three separate questions), where possible options included increase, decrease, or no change. For statistical analyses, they were transformed into binary variables, where '1' relates to the option chosen by the respondent and '0' relates to the opposite situation.

For the qualitative study, we have prepared a questionnaire, the scope of which encompasses not only the variables discussed above but also other constructs included in the conceptual framework (Figure 4.1). The structure of the questionnaire was organised around six themes emerging from this framework. For each theme, we have prepared a list of basic open-ended questions and an additional set of auxiliary, detailed questions, used when the answer provided was unclear or insufficiently comprehensive. After an introductory section aimed at defining the status of the participant in the firm and establishing the proper relationship for an in-depth interview, questions were asked to gather data related to (1) organisation, (2) external environment, (3) internationalisation strategy, (4) strategic importance and the professionalisation of personnel function, (5) HRM practices and their target groups, and (6) expectations and outcomes. At the closure, each participant was informed about the next steps of the research project, and asked for further contact in case of missing/ inconsistent/unclear data in the transcript of their interview.

4.3 Presentation of research procedure and samples

With regard to the quantitative research, the project covered internationalised SMEs located all over Poland. The empirical material was obtained from the survey conducted in the second quarter of 2021. The respondents of this study were founders/CEOs/top executives acting as

Table 4.1 Characteristics of the respondents in the quantitative study (N = 200)

Feature	Category	N	%
Status of respondent	(Co-)Owner	36	18.0%
	Managing Director	29	14.5%
	Member of Management Board	19	9.5%
	Senior Manager	74	37.0%
	HR Manager	42	21.0%
Gender	Female	70	35.0%
	Male	130	65.0%
Length of employment in the company	Shorter than 3 years[*]	19	9.5%
	3–5 years	47	23.5%
	6–9 years	50	25.0%
	10–14 years	39	19.5%
	15–19 years	19	9.5%
	20 years and longer	26	13.0%

Note
[*] In case of companies operating for less than three years, we accepted shorter length of employment, i.e. longer than a year.

single key informants representing Polish-based SMEs (Table 4.1). The procedure, preceded by the testing of the questionnaire, consisted of two stages: (1) the random selection of small and medium-sized exporting enterprises from the national database of GUS (Statistics Poland); (2) qualifying these entities for the study by telephone contact to apply two filtering questions. These questions were aimed at confirming that the company performs export activities and achieved at least the level of 25% FSTS. Out of 1395 selected firms, 308 (22.1%) did not meet the above criteria, while 887 (63.6%) refused to participate in the survey. It should be stressed that a major difficulty with regard to engaging key informants from these firms was related to Covid-19 challenges, as the second step of sampling procedure took place shortly after the peak of the third wave of the pandemic.

The final sample size (Table 4.2) was 200 with the overall response rate of 14.3%, which does not differ from the rates reported in prior empirical studies conducted in the internationalised SMEs (e.g. Isidor et al., 2011 had 10.6%; Ruzzier & Konecnik Ruzzier, 2015 had 13.5%; Vuorio et al., 2020 had 10%). Ninety-three entities met the requirements specified in our operational definition of EIFs adopted from Knight and Causvil (2004), i.e. achieving at least 25% FTST within a period of a maximum of three years since inception. The remaining 107 were exporting SMEs that internationalise at a slower pace, thus constituting a reference basis in the comparative analysis.

Table 4.2 Characteristics of the sample in the quantitative study (N = 200)

Feature	EIFs (N = 93)	Others (N = 107)	All (N = 200)
Industry (HT/non-HT)	37 (39.8%)/56 (60.2%)	46 (43%)/61 (57%)	83 (41.5%)/117 (58.5%)
Number of foreign markets M (SD)	11.85 (25.077)	10.64 (14.211)	11.21 (19.967)
Number of export areas M (SD)	1.98 (1.532)	2.07 (1.609)	2.03 (1.571)
Number of employees M (SD)	68.99 (71.562)	89.85 (71.859)	80.15 (72.297)
Age of the firm M (SD)	9.59 (9.841)	26.67 (23.039)	18.73 (20.011)
International experience M (SD)	8.73 (9.975)	16.96 (11.020)	13.14 (11.298)
Manufacturing/non-manufacturing	52 (55.9%)/41 (44.1%)	71 (66.3%)/36 (33.6%)	123 (61.5%)/77 (38.5%)
Family/non-family business	25 (26.9%)/68 (73.1%)	54 (50.5%)/53 (49.5%)	79 (39.5%)/121 (60.5%)
FSTS in % M (SD)	40.25 (19.845)	34.84 (13.914)	37.35 (17.102)
Regional/global scope	65 (69.9%)/28 (30.1%)	71 (66.4%)/36 (33.6%)	136 (68%)/64 (32%)
FDI/no FDI	21 (22.6%)/72 (77.4%)	26 (24.3%)/81 (75.7%)	47 (23.5%)/153 (76.5%)

To analyse quantitative data, we utilised several methods available in the IBM SPSS 28 software package. These included descriptive statistics; contingency tables with Chi2 test and post-hoc z-test with Bonferroni correction to compare proportions; regression analyses to test the impact of HRM practices on business and organisational outcomes; two-step clustering to identify emerging post-entry trajectories of internationalisation; ANOVA, t-test, and Mann-Whitney U test to compare means or ranks in groups. Findings of the quantitative studies are discussed in Section 5.2.

The qualitative study was conducted in the last quarter of 2021. This prolonged break between the two stages of our research project was an unavoidable consequence of another pandemic peak, which forced us to wait until the key informants were available and able to reflect on the past, current, and future situations of their businesses. The above situation caused some participants to withdraw their initial consent to face-to-face contact, instead offering a webcam interview via Skype, Teams, or Zoom. As a result, each webcam interview, approximately 80–90 minutes long, was videotaped and then transcribed.

The selection of interview participants was based on two criteria: (1) being a decision-maker familiar with HRM practices and international activity in a given company; (2) working in the given organisation for at least three years (Table 4.3). Importantly, at this step we focused on the early and rapid internationalisation of SMEs.

We selected eight case EIFs based on theoretical sampling (Eisenhardt & Graebner, 2007; Yin, 2013) because we found it to be the most suitable strategy for exploring the relationships between the constructs proposed in our conceptual framework and for addressing the research questions specified in Section 4.1. The case companies were derived from the database used in the first stage of our project. In order to be selected, they had to pass through several 'filters' applied sequentially. This procedure enabled us to ensure the sufficient sampling variability in terms of the contextual factors proposed in the conceptual model. However, guided by research questions, we primarily focused on internationalisation-related features so as to include various post-entry trajectories and challenges arising from them. Therefore, the selection started with identifying the set of SMEs compliant with the operational definition by Knight and Causvil (2004). We then distinguished between the regional (i.e. European) and global patterns followed by these firms. Within these two, we applied the second-order criterion concerning international commitment by foreign direct investment (apart from exporting). Consequently, out of the four emerging categories, we picked the case firms that varied in

Table 4.3 Characteristics of the case firms and their informants in the qualitative study

Criteria	Company A	Company B	Company C	Company D	Company E	Company F	Company G	Company H
Export areas other than Europe	Asia	Maghreb, other African countries	North America	no	no	Asia	no	Asia, Maghreb, North America
FDI	yes (Italy, production)	no	yes (sales & marketing, Germany, Switzerland, Austria, Czech Republic, France, USA)	no	no	yes (customer service, Germany)	yes (sales, Czech Republic, Slovakia)	no
FSTS in % (2020)	50	70	75	30	40	75	30	30
Number of foreign markets	three	ten	six	three	four	twelve	two	fifteen
International experience	5	5	6	3	5	12	13	23
Age of the firm	5	7	6	4	6	12	15	24
Employment size (2021)	45	51	46	13	100	150	210	80
Family business	yes	yes	no	yes	no	no	no	yes
Characteristics of the informant	Sales Manager	President of the management board	Key Account Manager	Founder and president of the management board	Co-owner	Manager of Logistics and Distribution	HR professional	HR Manager

terms of the extent of internationalisation (FSTS) and the organisational features (Table 4.3). Referring to the above criteria, it is worth noting the following points: firstly, it was not possible to use the differentiation of foreign markets as a criterion for selecting companies from the database prepared in the first stage of the project; secondly, in EIFs operating exclusively in Europe, the level of FSTS did not exceed 50%, thus the differentiation of cases in this respect concerns only global patterns.

Qualitative data in the form of interview transcripts were analysed in two stages: separately for each case, and then cross-sectional, which focused on the similarities and differences between cases compared according to the same schema (Yin, 2013, p. 225). For the purposes of the above analyses, the data was coded. We used different categories of such codes: closed, concerning constructs and their properties derived from the initial conceptual framework, and open, thematic, emerging from the collected material. Following the guidelines of O'Connor and Joffe (2020) on achieving satisfactory intercoder reliability, we developed definitions for these codes, applied them independently when coding the transcripts, then compared the results obtained by each member of our team, and repeated the procedure in the case of inconsistency. We have comprehensively discussed these findings in Sections 5.3 and 5.4.

Note

1 More specifically, we used fifty items relating to HRM practices, and three items concerning the innovation.

5 HRM practices in the investigated companies – empirical findings

5.1 Research context

In the previous chapters, we discussed issues related to the general context of SME functioning, the specificity of HRM in these types of organisations, and models of internationalisation. This section provides additional information about the context of SMEs in CEE countries and in Poland in particular. More specifically, it includes a brief presentation of the impact of the economic transformation process upon the development of entrepreneurship, the change in market conditions, and accessibility to foreign markets due to joining the EU, and changes in the approach to HRM in the region, which has altered mostly due to foreign investments in the region and the presence of international corporations in particular countries.

Business activity of SMEs in CEE countries has been developing dynamically in the last 30 years. It should be acknowledged that economic transformation, which took place in most countries of the region in the 1990s, was crucial for increasing entrepreneurship in the region. Previously, there were also small businesses run by entrepreneurs, but they did not receive support or were perceived to be crucial in national economies. The economic change resulted in a significant increase in the number of SMEs, which not only resulted from emerging opportunities but also from unemployment, which forced many people to seek alternative sources of income to contracted employment. During economic transformation, there were SMEs that started international cooperation but focused mainly on imports. Additionally, these companies faced many difficulties due to legal and tax issues as well as problems with transport and logistics.

The second important occurrence was the admission of eight countries from the region (including Poland) into the EU in 2004. It was a focal moment not only because SMEs got access to European

DOI: 10.4324/9781003319979-5

markets but also because of the number and value of EU programmes supporting these types of organisations. Since 2004, SMEs from CEE region have been beneficiaries of a number of programmes aimed at entrepreneurship support.

Additionally, entrepreneurial activity that started with the economic transition resulted also with the setting up of many family businesses in CEE countries. Currently, the key issue relating to the running of a family business is the succession process. A number of these businesses were set just after the collapse of the command economy and are run by nestors who are close to (or already at) retirement age. Thus, there is a need to pass the management of the firm to the next generation. According to the research of Polish Agency for Enterprise Development (2022) only 5% of family businesses in Poland are multigenerational. Thus, it can be concluded that in most CEE countries, family businesses face the process of succession for the first time. In other European countries, or in the USA, where entrepreneurship is much more embedded in the economy, such processes have been executed for decades.

In Poland, there is a special programme aimed at supporting family-owned SMEs in the succession process. It was started in 2018 and is implemented under the governance of PARP.

As previously mentioned, in CEE countries, the international activity of SMEs accelerated after the accession to the EU. Nevertheless, not all countries reported the same dynamics in the process of entering foreign markets. Additionally, some fluctuations occurred due to the situation on both domestic and foreign markets. When taking into account eight countries that accessed the EU in 2004, the level and the dynamics of the engagement of SMEs in export activities can be traced with the use of OECD data for the period of 2011–2019.

As far as small enterprises are concerned (Figure 5.1), in Estonia, Poland, and Slovenia, the number of small exporters has been increasing since 2011. However, it should be stressed that it is Poland that reports the highest growth in the number of these entities. In the Czech Republic, Lithuania, and Latvia, the number of exporting SMEs has remained stable since 2011. Negative trends referring to the decrease in the number of small exporters can be assigned to Hungary and Slovakia. In these countries, the number of such companies shrank after 2011 and in 2019 was again close to 2011.

In the case of medium exporters (Figure 5.2) the situation is similar to that concerning small entities. In Estonia, Slovenia, and Poland, the number of medium-sized exporters is rising but again, Poland reports the highest dynamics. Negative trends can be assigned to Slovakia, where the number of exporting medium enterprises in

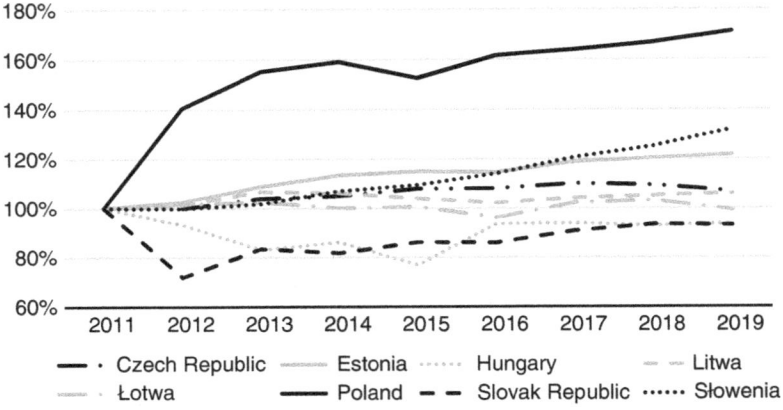

Figure 5.1 Trends in number of small exporting enterprises in countries that accessed the EU in 2004.

Source: OECD, 2022.

Note: For the Czech Republic, the share is calculated for 2012; the remaining countries relate to 2011. Due to missing data, the number of Estonian small exporters in 2018 was calculated as a mean of 2017 and 2019.

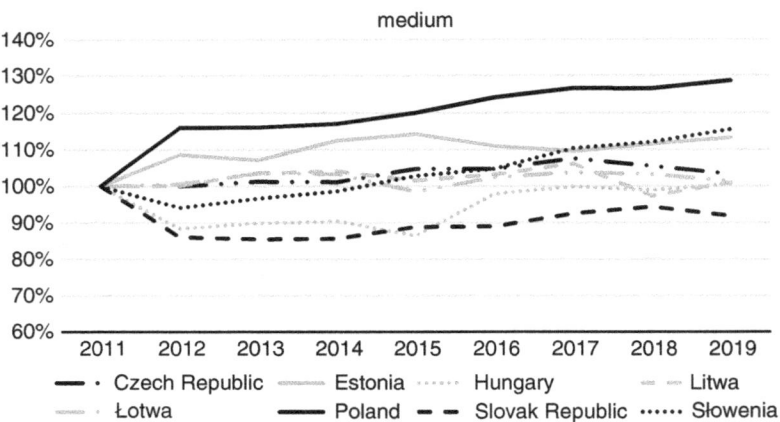

Figure 5.2 Trends in number of medium exporting enterprises in countries that accessed the EU in 2004.

Source: OECD, 2022.

Note: For Czech Republic the share is calculated for 2012; the remaining countries relate to 2011. Due to missing data, the number of Estonian medium exporters in 2018 was calculated as a mean of 2017 and 2019.

2019 was at the level of 90% of the quantity in 2011, with a drop to 86% between 2012 and 2014. In the remaining countries, despite some fluctuations, the number of medium-sized exporters have remained rather stable since 2011.

On the basis of the presented data, it can be concluded that in general, in most countries of the CEE region, the number of exporting SMEs is rather stable. However, Poland is an exception as the number of small and medium exporters has increased significantly since 2011.

A rise in the number of exporting SMEs was achieved, inter alia, thanks to the support of the Polish governmental and non-governmental institutions. The majority of initiatives were financed with EU funds, but there are also programmes that are financed solely by the Polish Government. Currently, there is a wide range of programmes that are aimed at supporting companies that want to enter foreign markets. According to data provided by the Ministry of Economic Development and Technology (2022), these programmes include:

- Substantive support for exporters (*Pomoc merytoryczna dla eksporterów*) – covers issues referring to the establishment of business relationships in other countries, access to databases with potential business partners and aid with legal procedures, taxes, and financial issues. This support is provided by trade chambers and diplomatic offices.
- Export financial support – this covers financial support in the case of the threat of unpaid invoices or help with loans for foreign trade partners that are to be used to import Polish goods.
- Foreign expansion fund – this is aimed at supporting companies that plan to open a branch abroad or buy an existing company in a foreign country (it supports FDI).
- Travel grants – these are offered only to SMEs that start cooperation with Norwegian companies. It covers the cost of travel and trade fairs.
- Internationalisation of Eastern Poland SMEs – this programme covers expenditures on promotion, employee training and the purchase of machinery required for internationalisation.
- Industry promotion programmes – these help in the promotion and branding of companies that operate in twelve industries with the highest export potential.

It should also be acknowledged that many Polish SMEs, as well as those from other CEE countries, received financial support for employees' training and development. In Poland, expenditures aimed at the development of competences were covered within two programmes – Human Capital (2007–2013) and Knowledge-Education-Development (2014–2020).

The HR function in Poland and in the CEEC region has undergone a significant transformation in the last 30 years as part of the transition process from the command economy to the market-based economy. Despite the different economic, socio-cultural, and historic backgrounds of various countries and organisations, a general trend of changes can be identified as the process of moving from personnel administration to human resource management, performed at the operating and strategic level, and increasingly often in the international dimension. During that time, old traditions often clashed with new challenges coming from a changing environment and enforcing organisations to develop a new approach to managing people, and redefine the role of the HR function. The aforementioned variety of contextual factors determining that process, moderates the observed impact and set some limits for generalisations. However, based on numerous publications, the following conclusions could be drawn: there is an increase of expertise in HRM resulting from research, education, consulting, and other HR services; the HR function plays an increasingly important role in organisations and is recognised as a business partner in the process of value delivery for stakeholders; the observed growing professionalism of HRM in general is not evenly distributed among different industries and companies. This last comment applies, inter alia, to SMEs in which HR practices often are specific and underdeveloped in comparison to large companies. In the last decade, the theory and practice of human resource management has been influenced by volatile and ambiguous contextual factors, which have led to turbulences on labour markets, and have subsequently been reflected in HRM policies and practices.

Recently, companies have been coped with influence of Covid-19 pandemic on their functioning, not least in the field of people management. The variety of protective policies implemented by national governments in order to slowdown and stop the transmission of coronavirus had negative consequences for nearly all companies, including international SMEs. Due to the slowdown and even the collapse of international transactions, logistics, and travel, many of these enterprises have faced crises-like difficulties. The abovementioned negative phenomenon caused by the Covid-19 pandemic has been strengthened by the war in Ukraine since February 2022. Besides the consequences of the pandemic and political factors, companies have been facing new simultaneous challenges coming from the digital transformation of work, the management of diversity, the development of sustainable HRM practices, the management of effectiveness and organisational resilience. All the aforementioned factors create a 'new normal' state of the art in the field of people management and determine how companies, including SMEs and early internationalised SMEs, need to adopt a new HR Ecosystem.

5.2 Analysis of quantitative results

We begin the discussion of findings with an overview of the contextual factors characterising early (EIFs) and late internationalised firms (LIFs). This enables us to capture the specifics of the former, which is a prerequisite to identify the sources of possible differences in human resource management arising from accelerated internationalisation. Consequently, the logical corollary of the above overview is a comparative analysis of HRM practices and their outcomes in both groups of internationalised SMEs. Based on this, we aim to determine whether EIFs become similar to late internationalisers in terms of managing human resources at the post-entry stage. Finally, bearing in mind the assumed diversity of EIF trajectories after entering foreign markets, we examine whether (and how) they constitute a source of intra-group differentiation in HRM practices.

Based on the data outlined in Table 4.2 (Section 4.3), we can notice a number of similarities between early and late internationalised SMEs, which include modest international involvement in the form of own foreign offices/branches/subsidiaries (approx. 23% of all cases); a moderate level of international complexity resulting from multiplicity of foreign markets (average: 11) and export regions (average: 2); the international scope predominantly limited to European countries (approx. 68% of all cases). Furthermore, the proportions of entities engaged in production as well as operating in the high-tech sector in both groups are similar (approx. 60% for EIFs and 40% for LIFs).

Statistical tests revealed significant differences between early and late internationalisers in terms of employment, age, international experience, the extent of internationalisation, and family involvement. More specifically, the former were significantly smaller (60 and 90 employees, respectively; $t = -2.052$, df: 198, $p = 0.041$), younger (10 and 27 years, respectively; $t = -6.641$, df: 198, $p < 0.001$), and were active internationally for a much shorter period (9 and 17 years, respectively; t: -5.505, df: 198, $p < 0.001$). Importantly, their extent of internationalisation was substantially higher (t: 2.252, df: 198, $p = 0.025$); more precisely, their average FSTS ratio exceeded 40, while for late internationalisers, it was less than 35. As for family businesses, the proportion of such companies amongst early internationalisers was substantially smaller in comparison to their late counter-partners (25% and 50%, respectively; Chi2 = 11.582, df: 1, p < 0.001).

To control the potential impact of factors related to the Covid-19 pandemic on HRM, we compared respondents' assessments of this influence on (1) employment; (2) wages; (3) training expenses in both groups. The distribution of responses did not differ significantly and the majority of respondents indicated no impact of the pandemic on the aforementioned issues. More precisely, for the EIFs, these proportions were 59%, 65%, and 58%, while for LIFs, they were 58%, 67%, and 71%, respectively. The percentage of companies reporting the negative effects of the pandemic did not exceed 28%.

Regarding HRM practices adopted by the investigated SMEs, we found that the proportions of early and late internationalisers with HR strategies (as separate documents or informal sets of goals/guidelines/priorities in this area) are almost identical. Specifically, such declarations stemmed from 59 (63.4%) and 67 (62.6%) respondents, respectively. Interestingly, EIFs and LIFs did not differ significantly in terms of the four base configurations of HRM practices (Figure 5.3). Moreover, the average utilisation levels of the aforementioned bundles are almost the same and represent a rather moderate 5-point value, i.e. approximately 70% of the maximum value of the measurement scale.

Nonetheless, differences between the compared groups appear when we consider individual questionnaire items relating to the detailed

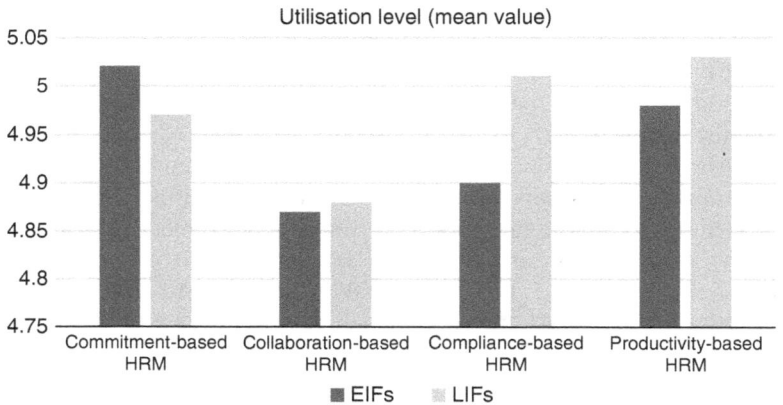

Figure 5.3 Four configurations of HRM practices used in early and late internationalised firms.

Note: The level of usage was measured using a 7-point Likert-type scale.

aspects of HRM (Table 5.1). Thus, in EIFs we found a significantly higher utilisation level of two practices assigned to the commitment-based model (i.e. employee autonomy in performing tasks and selection strategy), while in LIFs, higher use applied to some rewarding practices that belong to compliance-oriented and productivity-oriented configurations.

To compare HRM contribution to organisational and business outcomes in early and late internationalised SMEs, we applied four regression models (Tables 5.2, 5.3). Importantly, all these models were

Table 5.1 Differences in HRM practices between early and late internationalised firms – means, medians, and results of the Mann-Whitey U test

Items (shortened version)	EIFs	LIFs	Test statistics	p-value
jobs allow employees to routinely make changes in the way they perform them	4.86 (5)	4.21 (4)	6,004	0.011
recruitment focuses on selecting the best candidate regardless of the specific job	5.49 (6)	5.14 (5)	5,787.5	0.041
rewards are based on hourly pay	4.29 (4)	5.12 (5)	3,871.5	0.006
rewards value seniority	4.38 (4)	4.83 (5)	4,081	0.025

Table 5.2 Results of the ordered logit (dependent variable: sales growth) for EIFs and LIFs

Variable	EIFs		LIFs	
	β	Exp(β)	β	Exp(β)
HR strategy	0.796	1.451	0.105	1.111
Commitment-based HRM	−0.133	0.875	1.359***	3.891
Collaboration-based HRM	0.673*	1.960	0.584	1.793
Compliance-based HRM	0.442	1.556	0.302	1.352
Productivity-based HRM	0.025	1.026	−0.531	0.588
−2 Log-likelihood	210.939		205.669	
GoF (Pearson's Chi2)	376.041	p = 0.212	493.160	p = 0.103
Pseudo R^2 (Cox & Snell)	0.176		0.331	
Pseudo R^2 (Nagelkerke)	0.191		0.366	
R^2 (McFadden)	0.077		0.170	
Model χ^2	17.601**		42.265***	

Note: Level of significance: *p < 0.05; **p < 0.01; ***p < 0.001.

Table 5.3 Results of linear regression (dependent variable: firm innovation) for EIFs and LIFs

Variable	EIFs	LIFs
	β	β
HR strategy	−0.063	0.070
Commitment-based HRM	0.351**	0.385***
Collaboration-based HRM	0.525***	0.475***
Compliance-based HRM	0.034	0.062
Productivity-based HRM	−0.060	−0.072
R^2	0.597	0.592
Adjusted R^2	0.574	0.571
F	25.749***	29.250***

Note: Level of significance: **$p < 0.01$; ***$p < 0.001$. Values of beta coefficients are standardised.

fitted to the empirical data. Ordinal regression analyses show that EIFs and LIFs differ in terms of the relationships between HRM practices and their business outcomes (Table 5.2). More specifically, in EIFs with the increasing use (by a unit) of collaboration-based HRM practices, the odds of a higher level of sales growth are 1.96 times greater, while amongst late internationalisers, such a positive contribution refers to the commitment-based configuration, for which these odds are 3.981 times greater.

Based on linear regressions, we found that in both categories of SMEs, the same bundles of practices, namely collaboration-based and commitment-based configurations, significantly contribute to a firm's innovation (Table 5.3).

The final aspect of our considerations is the emerging patterns of early internationalised SMEs and the corresponding approaches to HRM. Thus, to identify the above trajectories, we applied two-step clustering based on three variables – the scope, the forms, and the extent of international activity – which resulted in three categories of EIFs (Table 5.4).

The most numerous cluster relates to European Exporters comprising smaller entities with an average ratio of foreign sales reaching 34%, operating in a few foreign markets. The second largest cluster consists of companies acting as International Investors in many foreign countries (average: 26 countries) in a global or regional scale. Global Exporters mostly represent medium-sized manufacturing firms that are more involved in overseas sales (with FSTS of 50.8%) and face much greater international complexity than their regional counter-partners.

Table 5.4 Similarities and differences between the three clusters of early internationalised SMEs

Feature	European exporters (N = 55)	International investors (N = 21)	Global exporters (N = 17)
FDI***	0^a	21^b (100%)	0^a
Global scope***	0^a	11^b (52%)	17^c (100%)
FSTS*	34.2^L	47.6^H	50.8^H
Number of foreign markets*	4.31^L	26.05^H	18.71^H
Number of export areas***	1.2^L	2.95^H	3.29^H
Number of employees***	44.5^L	112.6^H	94.4^H
Manufacturing activity*	26^a (47.3%)	$12^{a,b}$ (57.1%)	14^b (82.4%)
HR strategy***	25^a (45.5%)	18^b (85.7%)	16^b (94.1%)
Commitment-based HRM**	4.57^L	4.96	5.29^H
Collaboration-based HRM*	4.66^L	5.03	5.35^H
Compliance-based HRM	4.79	5.10	5.01
Productivity-based HRM**	4.74^L	5.26^H	5.39^H

Notes

L   denotes significantly lower while.

H   denotes significantly higher mean value in post-hoc Hochberg test.

a   Letters in the subscript represent categories of the EIFs for which column proportions do not differ significantly from each other at $p < 0.05$.

b   Letters in the subscript represent categories of the EIFs for which column proportions do not differ significantly from each other at $p < 0.05$.

c   Letters in the subscript represent categories of the EIFs for which column proportions do not differ significantly from each other at $p < 0.05$.

*   significant at $p < 0.05$ (ANOVA, df: 2, F value for FSTS: 7.235; Number of foreign markets: 7.389; Collaboration-based HRM: 3.168; Chi2 = 6.5, df: 2, for manufacturing).

**   significant at $p < 0.01$ (ANOVA, df: 2, F value for Commitment-based HRM: 5.035; Productivity-based HRM: 6.849).

***   significant at $p < 0.001$ (Chi2=93, df: 2 for FDI; Chi2 = 68.108, df: 2 for Global scope; Chi2 = 19.061, df: 2 for HR Strategy; ANOVA, df: 2, F value for Number of employees: 9.767; Number of export areas: 27.914).

As expected, these three categories of EIFs adopted different HRM practices that can be explained by the specific challenges arising from their post-entry internationalisation. First, our findings demonstrate that most European Exporters do not have an HR strategy, which sharply contrasts with practices reported in two other clusters (i.e. 54.5% of the former compared to 14.3% of International Investors, and 5.9% of Global Exporters). Secondly, based on Hochberg post-hoc tests preceded by ANOVA, we found significant differences between the clusters referring to the usage of commitment-, collaboration-, and productivity-based configurations of HRM practices, which was in general lower amongst European Exporters than in other categories of EIFs (Table 5.4).

This research also revealed diverse patterns of using these bundles of practices. In particular, both European Exporters and International Investors more eagerly reached for compliance and productivity-oriented practices, while Global Exporters adopted collaboration-, commitment-, and productivity-based configurations. Additionally, we tested the differences between the categories of EIFs with regard to detailed HRM practices (i.e. a total of 50 items adopted from Lepak and Snell (2002), that belong to five HR domains presented in Figure 5.4). As a result, we found that the only HR area in which the respondents' answers did not differ significantly is compensation/rewards. In other domains (i.e. work design, recruitment and selection, training and development as well as employee appraisal) the utilisation levels of individual practices indicated by European Exporters were clearly lower than those of other clusters (Figure 5.4). The differences between International Investors and Global Exporters turned out to be insignificant; however, due to their smaller number, this result should be treated as only preliminary.

Regarding firm innovation, no differences between the clusters were found. The level of the above outcome ranged from 4.95 in the largest group to 5.49 for International Investors. With regard to sales growth, the results of non-parametric tests (Kruskal-Wallis test statistics: 7.724,

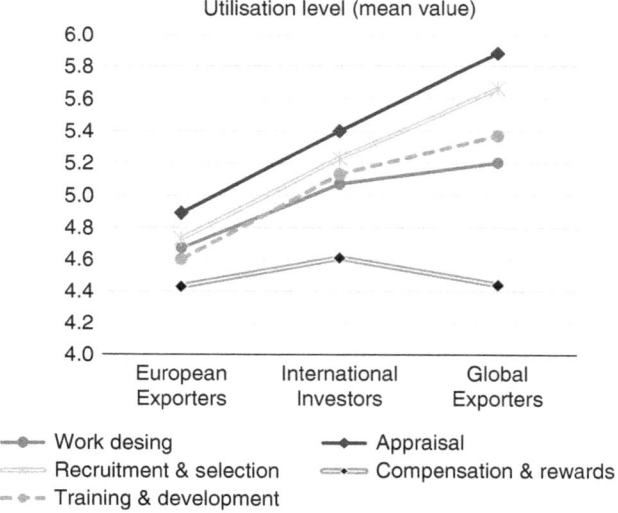

Figure 5.4 The use of HRM practices aggregated into five main HR domains according to categories of EIFs.

Note: The level of usage was measured using a 7-point Likert-type scale.

df: 2, p = 0.021, Median test statistics: 11.621, df: 2, p = 0.003) showed differences between European Exporters and two other groups, in favour of the latter.

Summing up the quantitative research, it can be initially stated that a "typical" early internationalised company rarely operates as a family business, usually employs several dozen people, and has been present on the international market for just a few to around 12 years. Most often, it conducts export activities in several European countries, occasionally reaching for equity entry modes.

The comparative analysis of HRM practices revealed several features common to early and late internationalised SMEs, such as a similar proportion of companies having HR strategies, a similar level of use of four core configurations of practices, and a positive impact of the collaboration and commitment-oriented approaches on firm innovation. However, after disaggregating these configurations, it turned out that EIFs and LIFs differ in their application of some work design, recruitment, and rewarding policies. We also found that the considered bundles of HRM practices work differently in the compared groups in terms of their contribution to business outcomes.

Simultaneously, the use of HRM core bundles, as well as the strategic importance of the personnel function, shows substantial differentiation depending on the pattern of development among early internationalisers. The results of this study suggest that developing HR strategy and methods of conducting HRM activities becomes more important when companies in the post-entry phase experience higher international complexity arising from operating beyond European markets and/or greater involvement in foreign markets through direct investment.

5.3 Presentation of case studies

5.3.1 The business environment and internationalisation process in the investigated companies

In Section 4.3, the general characteristics of the companies chosen for qualitative research were presented. These companies vary in terms of business sector, size, ownership, age, and experience on international markets. Nevertheless, all respondents from these companies claimed that the business environment is of high importance in their functioning. They stated that in general, the conditions under which they operate are more dynamic and complex than before. Most challenges stem from customers' expectations and changes in technology. However, *Company A* stated that access to materials and components may cause real difficulties in achieving production objectives. Almost all of the investigated companies claimed to adjust to the changes in an incremental way. Only *Company D* stated that sometimes they had to adapt by undertaking radical actions, and *Company F* claimed its adjustment is mostly ad-hoc. The scope of adjustment covers technical improvements (*Companies B, E, F,* and *H*), product/service modifications (*Companies A, C, D,* and *G*) and in some cases the customer care process (*Companies C* and *G*).

Most companies (six out of eight) planned to operate internationally from their inception. It was the owner's strategic goal to enter foreign markets and operate internationally. In the case of *Companies E, G,* and *H,* the international activity resulted from previous business. The international activity started by direct contacts with potential partners abroad (*Companies A, B,* and *C*), but some companies also conducted market research (*D, E*) or took part in fairs (*A, B*). In the case of *Company G,* the regional offices in two other countries were set to acquire customers. Similarly, *Company A* hired an experienced salesman to launch products on foreign markets. *Company F* started with cooperation with other Polish firms which were operating internationally. On the basis of this cooperation, they also started offering their services internationally. *Company H* started with importing products necessary for the production and then on the basis of set relationships, they developed new networks enabling export.

For each company, foreign markets are perceived to be crucial in their business activities. Most of their income is obtained from abroad. Three companies (*B, D, G*) stated that their current market situation is better than that of their competitors. *Companies A* and *C* claimed that their situation is stable and they face rather no competition from other firms. Respondents from *Companies F* and *H* perceive their situation to be similar to other firms and only an interviewee from *Company E* claimed that their company is in the entry phase, facing strong competition, which makes their position rather weak.

Most companies plan to increase their involvement in foreign markets by entering new markets, increasing the sales level, and acquiring new customers. Only two companies have not planned a strong development on foreign markets: *Company G* is focused on maintaining their existence abroad and does not plan to enter new countries; *Company H* must deal with covid restrictions and faces currency exchange rates, which limits their market potential. Similarly, *Company A* has to face such Covid-19 consequences as collapse of the supply chain or higher absenteeism. For *Company C,* the Covid-19 situation meant a sales decrease which has been already restored. Moreover, two companies (*F, H*) have withdrawn from Belarus and Russia.

5.3.2 *Human Resource Management in investigated companies*

Company A

Human resource management is handled by the company's managing director and department managers, while the handling of employee matters, such as payroll administration, is carried out by an external company. A key success factor and at the same time a challenge in HRM is to have competent people with the right knowledge and skills.

> *From the beginning, it was clear that, for example, sales employees must know foreign languages and have the ability to easily interact with people, talk, and so on. It is clear that we do not require the same competencies from fitters who need to know the technical procedures perfectly.*
>
> *Sales manager*

New job positions are created for the development needs of the company. In the process of recruiting employees, we use both employment agencies and advertisements on the Internet. The selection process includes telephone interviewing, resume analysis, and face-to-face meetings with job candidates. As part of the onboarding of newly hired employees, we use instruction and training in the departments to which the people were recruited and tasks to be performed. The supervision of the process is exercised by department managers.

The results achieved by employees are discussed among the management team and used in determining annual bonuses or in the promotion of employees. Such criteria as 'employees' commitment to work and the company's development are considered, as is absenteeism statistics.

Training activities include training, courses, or the participation in trade fairs. Some of them have these forms of activities carried out regularly, while some of them depend on current needs. The addressees of these activities are managers from various departments: technical, purchasing, and sales. In the case of manual workers, training is also conducted, such as courses to update their skills or formal qualifications, e.g. in the profession of an electrician. Training needs are assessed based on the observations of work, the results obtained or discussions with managers. Employees can also report their training needs.

Remuneration includes a fixed part and a variable part in the form of individual bonuses. These are linked to the performance of individual employees and the financial condition of the company.

Due to a low employee turnover rate, the company has not developed a procedure for managing layoffs.

Key employees are characterised by knowledge and experience. They are able to carry out certain tasks which other employees can't. The most important competences are sales, purchasing, and technical skills. In the opinion of the representative of the company, the competency level of employees in the field of international activities is good and is successively improving with every project.

The respondent was not able to express an opinion about the effectiveness of HR activities – the only comment was that there are no issues in this field, and that no changes were introduced in recent years. However, the implementation of some product innovations was reported.

The overall condition and the market position of the firm are good.

Company B

In this company there is no HRM strategy or HR department. There is a person responsible for administrative duties, referring to payroll and employment-related documentation. HRM activities are executed by line managers. Most tasks are assigned to particular job positions but there are also emerging duties which are delegated to particular employees according to the needs and workload. In this company, there are no structured job descriptions. In general, tasks for basic positions are defined by line managers.

> *Employees have their tasks defined to some extent. However, their duties are very wide. You know … they have their daily routines but potentially they may do something else. It is the manager's role to assign activities.*
>
> *President of the management board*

There is no employment planning – staffing is conducted when a particular need arises. In such a case, the company runs recruitment process on its own or uses an external recruitment agency. Selection is based on CV screening and interviews. No onboarding programmes are developed, only the trial employment contract is introduced. To evaluate employees, only work outcomes are taken into account. On the basis of goal achievement, the level of bonuses is calculated. Development is not structured or planned. When a particular need arises and the gap in competences is identified, training is planned and then introduced. Such training is not obligatory; however, any employee may take part in it.

Remuneration system consists of three components: basic salary, performance-based bonuses, and annual reward. The latter can be received only by a limited number of employees.

There are no activities undertaken towards employees that quit or are dismissed. Additionally, there are no specific regulations introduced with regard to employees engaged in the firm's international operations.

Key employees are those who have a high level of competences, experience, and engagement in task fulfilment.

The most important competences are fluency in English, the ability to set and maintain relationships, and the knowledge about the firm and its products. These competences are evaluated to be at the average level among the employees.

In this company, there are no structured HR-related procedures or processes. Some people-management practices are executed by managers and, according to the respondent's opinion, they are run in a sufficient manner. However, as the interviewee claimed, there is always something to be improved. Within the last two years, no modifications or changes in HR practices were introduced. However, innovation in the internal processes referring to management was launched.

According to the respondent's opinion, the firm performs better than its counterparts in the branch in such areas as level of income, market share, cost optimisation or launching new products, services, or innovations. In general the overall firm's condition is better than that of other firms.

Company C

Human resource management is carried out by an external HR agency that proposes solutions to the company's president with regard to HR matters.

> *The company's policy is that in any foreign market, HR and payroll matters are handled by an external company that is most familiar with the local law.* Decisions are made solely by the company's president.
>
> *Key account manager*

The scopes of tasks are not formally defined.

> *Everyone knows what to do. No one gets in anyone's way. Everyone is responsible for their own tasks, and we usually occupy independent positions.*
>
> *Key account manager*

The company has the requirement profiles for ideal job candidates used in the recruitment and selection processes. These processes are not carried out on a regular basis as the company has a stable workforce, and it seeks new employees only in the event of increased demand for its services, such as the need to implement more systems than usual.

In the recruitment process, recommendations from current employees are used first, followed by the placement of advertisements on portals on the Internet. During the selection process, an interview is conducted to identify the skills and motivations for taking the job. Newly hired employees then undergo a six-month onboarding period.

Neither the evaluation of employees nor assessment of the effects or quality of their work is carried out. The only evaluation is customer satisfaction.

Training sessions are held twice a month and take the form of remote meetings to discuss news and changes. They are addressed to all employees, with only salespeople are obliged to attend. Training needs are determined based on customer requests and changes to programs developed in-house.

The training is conducted by a programmer and a marketer.

Salaries consist of a base part indexed in January against inflation and a Christmas bonus. Their size is determined by the position held, the scope of duties, and the working time.

There are no developed practices for managing employees who leave the company due to low turnover rate.

There are no specific HR solutions referring to the international activities of the company. There are no key employees – all of them are equally important. The most important competences are sales skills.

In the field of HRM, no real issues were reported. There have also not been any modifications introduced within the last years. In comparison, some process innovations in the field of customer service were introduced, e.g. logistic terminals or implementation fees. The firm's condition in the areas of sale's dynamics and profitability was similar and even better than by other firms on the market, whereas the market share went down a little. In the respondent's opinion, in crisis times, some customers look for less expensive products. This happens in rather a short time period, and then customers come back. The overall firm's conditions are good.

Company D

One person is responsible for the handling of employee matters. Decisions are made by the company's president and he also determines the direction of development.

Duties are defined in the employment contract. They are broad and quite similar for most jobs. The requirements for job candidates are based on the specifics of the projects implemented. They form the basis of the recruitment process, which is performed mainly in the form of advertisements on job portals, sometimes through employment agencies. The selection process includes a resume analysis and an interview, which is conducted by the company's president or his wife, who is a member of the board. Onboarding is carried out under the supervision of the president.

The evaluation of employees takes the form of ongoing observations of their commitment to their work. Absenteeism is also taken into account. The results of the ongoing evaluation are considered for bonuses.

Training courses are conducted regularly and addressed to all employees. They include both substantive job-related content as well as other general development content.

> *We have a training package, but also as a company taking to heart the slogan "a sound mind in a sound body", we take care of our employees' fitness and use a system of gym benefits.*
> *Founder and president of the management board*

Training is provided by external firms. Employees can make suggestions in this regard.

Remuneration consists of a basic salary, resulting from the employment contract, and an individual bonus or a team bonus that the leader distributes to team members.

There are no developed formal procedures for employees who leave company. Such cases are rare and, if they do occur, are related to changes in a family situation or a place of residence.

According to the opinion of the founder and president of the company, every employee is equally important.

> *For me every employee is a key employee. Our company is a small team and ever employee is a part of this organism. In case we lose an employee, it will not be easy to find someone for replacement, to train and additionally to trust. Trust is very important.*
> *Founder and president of the management board*

The most important competences are fluency in English and sales skills.

Expanding business in foreign markets does not involve making changes in the HRM area.

Goals in the field of HRM are accomplished and there are no real issues here, so there has been no need for modifications within recent years.

Innovations regarding internet platforms are continuously modernised, thus making them more attractive for users.

The financial situation of the firm as well as employment is good, and it is increasingly visible on the market from year to year.

Company E

HR matters are handled by the human resources department and partly by the accounting department.

> *We call them "staff and payroll". They handle employee matters, as well as support managers. There is even one person from Ukraine in this department as production employs workers from Ukraine, Belarus, and Kazakhstan. The department comprehensively handles all HR processes and cooperates with external entities.*
>
> *Co-owner*

Personnel decisions are made by department managers and the owners. There is no HRM strategy but a practice of on-going planning is applied according to order bundles and production capacity.

Employees have specific responsibilities and rights in their employment contracts. Competency requirements for jobs are defined and form the basis of employee recruitment and selection processes. Recruitment uses local Internet portals and employment offices. The selection process includes the analysis of documents and interviews in a traditional or an online form. They are attended by department managers in addition to an HR specialist. The first contract is signed for three months, which is a probationary period.

Periodic evaluations are used at least once per year. Evaluations include commitment, absenteeism, and specific indicators in particular departments, e.g. in the sales department, they are concerned with the timeliness of orders. Assessments are conducted by department managers, while the managers are evaluated by the company's management.

Employee development is performed in the form of training, which is carried out according to current needs and opportunities. They are conducted by external companies and sometimes information and training materials are prepared by internal units such as the accounting department.

Remuneration consists of a basic salary and an annual bonus paid in December.

As for periods of employee leave, there are no special procedures for handling them. The turnover is high among employees from Ukraine.

The most important individuals in the company are experienced managers who have worked for the company from its beginning. Apart from that, fluency in English and sales skills are crucial competences.

There is one HR issue the company copes with and it is the attraction and retention of production workers, caused not least by shortages on the labour market. In recent years, no modifications regarding HRM practices were introduced. A challenging innovation was the rearrangement of some departments to remote work. The overall condition of the firm is good and stays at the same level, despite turbulences in the areas of supply, sale, or cost. The market share remains small.

Company F

The company does not have an HR strategy and does not plan any HR-related activities. In the HR department, there are two employees responsible mainly for payroll and administrative issues.

In general, jobs are well structured, employees have a scope of roles and activities. Job descriptions are not modified or updated frequently. When signing a job contract, the employee accepts the scope of tasks and it remains unchanged.

In general, there are no problems with retention, there are hardly any resignations. When there is a need to employ someone, line managers are responsible for the process. They publish job advertisements and then run screening and conduct job interviews. A positively verified candidate is invited for a trial day, during which, they become familiar with duties, the team, and the organisation. If there is a will to cooperate, a three-month trial contract is signed. New employee is trained by a supervisor, the training covers internal processes and the firm's IT systems. There is a performance-based appraisal system which is executed monthly. Each employee is evaluated by a supervisor. Additionally, the workflow is monitored and in case of any derogations, feedback is provided.

> *We analyse performance monthly to assure the flow, to provide services to any customer. During the interview, we consider why on particular routes there was no transport, why someone's outcomes have dropped and if there is a way to overcome such difficulties, we immediately undertake actions; if not, we consider how to prevent such situations in the future. … Moreover, work is constantly monitored by supervisors and if there is a need, direct feedback is provided.*
> *Manager of logistics and distribution*

Training is provided for every employee when a particular need arises. The company does not run planned development programmes. However, when someone faces difficulties dealing with tasks, individual training initiatives are provided. Each employee receives a basic salary and a provision-based monthly bonus.

There are no specific competences required from the employees. However, haulers must be familiar with the legal regulations of particular countries. No specific activities towards employees engaged in international activities were introduced.

Goals in the field of HRM are accomplished in a sufficient manner. The introduced tools and procedures strongly support line managers in dealing with people-related activities. Within the last two years, no changes or modifications in HR processes have been introduced.

No products, services, or process innovations have been introduced in the last two years.

It is the respondent's opinion that dynamics of income, market share, cost optimisation, and the launch of new products, services, or innovations, are at the same level as in the other companies in the branch.

Company G

There is an HR strategy that was created on the basis of business goals. The scope of duties of the HR department covers recruitment, development, payroll, and other activities related to current needs. There are also HR Business Partner posts, and people employed in such positions support line managers in HR-related issues. Moreover, they gather information which is analysed and used to create strategic and operational plans in the HR field.

There are precisely defined job descriptions developed on the basis of job demands, work breakdown, and observations. Tasks and duties are structured to a high extent. Modifications are seldom introduced, potential changes apply to top positions only.

Staffing is executed when particular needs arise (for example because of resignations or changes in job position). In recruitment, the company applies publishing job advertisements, a referrals program, and the support of external recruitment agencies. With regard to basic positions, simple methods are applied, but in the case of top positions, cooperation with external HR agencies is chosen. The selection process varies between positions and includes screening, interviews, knowledge tests, and other forms of selection.

We recruit in any form possible to succeed. We cannot rely solely on one method. For sure, there are job advertisements that we publish, we use employee referrals, and also we cooperate with recruitment agencies. As far as selection is concerned, it also depends on the post. For a basic position there is a screening process executed first by an internal recruiter, then initially selected offers are transferred to a direct supervisor who runs a second round of screening. Selected candidates are invited for an interview. In the case of technical positions, additional tests covering particular areas of knowledge are applied. With regard to top positions, we rely on the tools applied by the external agencies we cooperate with.

HR professional

The onboarding programme covers the introduction to the team, the presentation of the company, on-the-job initial training, Health and Safety (H&S) training, and the presentation of general rules and procedures.

Each employee has a set of individual goals. These are based on job position and various measures of performance are implemented depending on the department. The level of goal accomplishment is evaluated quarterly and a general appraisal is then conducted annually. For every employee, the process is the same, and the differences refer only to the scope of goals and their measures. The results of the appraisal are used in making decisions with regard to promotion, training, and rewards.

There is a training team which prepares yearly development plans. For basic positions, training is conducted by internal trainers. For technical specialists and employees in top positions, training is conducted by external providers. Development programmes cover a wide range of competences such as dealing with customers, problem-solving, and also team management or topics referring to specific technical knowledge.

The remuneration system includes basic salary and post-referral components, for example: for sales team employees, there is commission; for technical employees, the bonus is calculated on the basis of services provided; leaders or managers may receive extra bonuses based on the performance of their teams.

In case of group layoffs, the firm provides outplacement programmes. These programmes are supported by external HR agencies. In other cases, there is an exit questionnaire aimed at gathering information about the reasons behind quitting the job.

HR-related activities are evaluated as being good. However, it is the respondent's opinion that there is always something to be improved. In the last two years, some changes in HR administration and documentation have been introduced. They refer to digitalisation and the introduction of some IT solutions in the field of HR administration.

No products or service innovations have been introduced within the last two years. However, the company modified and improved internal communication as well as communication with customers. This also encompasses the purchase of new equipment and modification in the IT infrastructure.

In the respondent's opinion, the firm performs better than its competitors in the following areas: dynamics of income, market share, cost optimisation, and the launch of new products, services, or innovations.

Company H

In this company, there is an HR department responsible mostly for administrative issues. There is no written HRM strategy – all activities are planned by the owner who decides which of them should be introduced and when. The HR department does not support line managers in dealing with day-to-day employee management.

Every employee has a precisely defined job description with exact tasks and duties. These are included in the job contract which is signed when hiring. Job descriptions are seldom changed – the last modification was introduced during the covid pandemic and referred to the implementation of remote work.

The recruitment process is rarely conducted and there are no problems with retention in the firm. If there is a need to employ, a line manager provides the HR department with requirements. A job advertisement is then published. After collecting offers, a selection process including screening and interviews is executed. Employees are hired for a trial period, starting with H&S training and a presentation of the firm and its structure.

Employee evaluation is based on efficiency, absenteeism, and quality level. An appraisal is conducted by supervisors once a year and on its basis, a decision about rewards is made.

Development programmes are designed mostly for administrative departments. Development covers mainly obligatory training (aimed at obtaining remits and providing actual knowledge). It is mostly executed by external providers. The number of training courses has decreased over the last two years.

Previously, every employee had at least one training course per year – recently most of them have been conducted on-line, thus we conduct less training. These programmes were dedicated mostly to administration rather than production employees. If these are H&S topics, the training is conducted by an expert, if these are issues referring to taxes, it is organised by external providers,

HR manager

Remuneration system consists of two components – basic salary and bonuses. Bonuses are calculated by the managers on the basis of performance evaluation.

There are no activities undertaken towards employees resigning or being dismissed. The are no specific activities developed for employees engaged in the firm's international activity. The crucial employees competences encompass engagement and identification with the firm.

No real HR issues are reported. Within the last two years, no changes in HR processes have been introduced. Some modifications that have been made referred to remote work requirements.

The firm have introduced some product innovations. However, due to the business profile, such improvements are made regularly.

It is the respondent's opinion that dynamics of income, market share, cost optimisation, and the launch of new products, services, or innovations are at the same level as in other companies in the branch.

5.4 Cross-case analysis

In this section, similarities and differences in the HRM of the above-presented case studies are analysed. First, some strategic and organisational issues in the area of HRM are introduced, then HR practices and their configurations are described; finally, HR and other outcomes are depicted.

The main actors in the field of HRM in the cases described earlier are company directors, line managers, internal HR specialists, and external HR agencies. In all cases, owners/managing directors are in charge of HRM decisions. In some companies, line managers are involved in that process (A, B, F). In most of the analysed cases, no written or formalised HRM strategy is identified. Only in one firm (G) are planning activities in the field of HRM reported, and in another firm (H), the existence of an unwritten form of HR strategy is mentioned. Administrative HR issues such as payroll, training, and recruitment are carried out internally by an HR specialist/department (B, D, E, F, G, H) or outsourced (A, C). Additionally Company G is a post of HR Business Partner as support for line managers. The existence of an HR department is noted in middle-sized companies (E, F, G, H), with the number of employees being between 80 and 210.

In all companies, key employees are recognised as strategic assets, even when the term 'key employee' is not used (E, H). Most often, highlighted features which characterised these employees are experience (A, B, E, G, H) and knowledge (A, B, G, H). Besides these characteristics of key employees, two others were mentioned, namely engagement (C, G) and having an important position or role in the company (F, H). There are no formal dedicated HR practices addressed to these employees.

Expanding business in foreign markets does not involve making crucial changes in HRM practices in all of the described cases. Reasons that are declared for such an approach include no differences between activities in domestic and foreign markets (D) or the responsibility for HR issues by an external company (C). There is only one issue raised by some companies in connection with the internationalisation, namely improving knowledge in English (B, E, F, G).

In almost all of the investigated companies (except one), employees' tasks and duties are precisely defined and structured. They are a part of a job contract, and are signed upon employment. According to respondents' claims, these tasks and duties have remained unchanged since the beginning of their employment. The only modifications that have been introduced stemmed from covid regulations and the introduction of remote working. Thus, it can be concluded that in the investigated companies, the level of job specialisation and structurisation is very high. Such an approach results in a lack of job rotation, which in large organisations is perceived as an effective tool for competency development. According to respondents, if any position change occurs, it is due to sick leave and refers only to blue collars.

On the basis of information gathered, it can be stated that in investigated companies, there is a very high level of employee retention. Almost all companies claimed that recruitment activities are undertaken sporadically if there is an unexpected increase in the products/ services sale volume or in the case of when someone quits, which happens occasionally. Recruitment processes cover mostly production or salesforce employees rather than those who are in charge of administrative/office duties. In these companies, regardless of the level of reported business outcomes, the conviction that they have a well-prepared and stable workforce dominates.

Among the investigated firms, three approaches in defining expectations towards potential employees can be defined. The first refers to job descriptions – a candidate profile based on a precisely defined scope of tasks, duties, and competences is included in job descriptions. This approach is applied in Companies F and G which operate in services are relatively old (12 and 15 years respectively) and have operated on international markets for more than ten years. According to the second approach, expectations towards candidates are defined by line managers. It is their duty to define what kind of knowledge, skills, and abilities a candidate should possess. This model is applied in Companies A, E, and H, which are of a production profile. In the third approach, a candidate's profile is defined on the basis of future and potential tasks to be fulfilled and is created ad-hoc when a particular need to recruit someone arises. This refers to Companies B, C, and D, which are relatively young (4–7 years) and have been operating on international markets for 3–5 years.

All companies confirmed that they use job-related portals in the Internet to place job advertisements. Additionally, three companies cooperate with recruitment agencies, and three use employees' referrals. Only one company claimed that it applies a variety of recruitment techniques and channels, which are crafted for a particular position and make it possible to hire an appropriate candidate. This refers to Company G which has the highest employment level (among the investigated companies) and has existed for more than 15 years. Among the investigated companies, six claimed that they apply the same recruitment techniques regardless of position, and two (A and H), which operate in production, differentiate recruitment techniques with regard to production and non-production employees.

During the candidates' evaluation process, all companies apply CV analysis and job interviews. Additionally, two companies (E and G) have declared that they apply some competency tests to evaluate the level of particular competences. This refers to specialist posts and enables the verification of, for example, technical aptitude and the knowledge of IT programmes. These two companies claimed to achieve an increase in sales in the years 2018–2020.

Five companies (A, C, F, G, H) declared that they run onboarding programmes. These include the firm's presentation, H&S training, and presentation of the particular departments' scope of duties. However, there is no common approach in the duration of this process. Some companies claim that all onboarding activities are executed during one day or a few days (F, G, H) while in other companies, it lasts from one to even six months (A, C) in the case of some posts for which detailed knowledge about products, services, and processes is required.

On the basis of this information, it can be concluded that the process of employee acquisition is run with the use of basic tools and is executed in a simplified way. Job advertisements placed on the Internet are used to acquire candidates, they are then assessed during screening and job interviews, and onboarding covers basic issues in most cases. However, all companies confirmed that they hire employees for a trial period – which lasts from one to three months – during which they evaluate whether the candidate meets expectations.

Only three companies declare they have a performance management system (F, G, H). Others claimed that although they have not introduced the system, they monitor the level of goal achievement in an ongoing manner. Among the investigated companies, there tend to be no similarities with regard to the appraisal system. Some companies declare they evaluate employees monthly (B, F), while others do so quarterly or yearly (A, E, G). Specified tools, which would enable the execution of the evaluation process, are not developed and introduced. The evaluation is conducted in some cases by the line manager while in others, it is performed by the owner. However, what is common in these organisations is a strong focus on performance. All respondents claimed that this is the level of sales or production which is taken into account when evaluating employees. Additionally, some companies (A, G) include levels of engagement and absenteeism in the evaluation. Nevertheless, none of investigated companies declared that they assess employees' competences.

All companies declared they run training, and every employee may take part in it. However, some groups of employees are provided with more training than others. In general, there are more activities aimed at white rather than blue collars. Development programmes refer to the issues which directly correspond to performance and task execution. They encompass, for example, changes in products for salesforce, new technologies for specialists and production workers, and changes in legal or financial regulations for office workers. If training covers changes in products or services, it is executed by managers or specialists. If training refers to H&S issues or changes in legal regulations, it is executed by an external provider.

In the investigated companies, there are no structured activities referring to the assessment of training needs or planning the development of employees. Respondents claimed that all actions aimed at the development of competences are undertaken when a particular need arises. None of the firms confirmed the execution of training aimed at the development of interpersonal, social, or teamwork competences. Thus, it can be concluded that all developmental activities are run only when they are obligatory (H&S for example) or necessary to assure the expected quality of the internal process or to ensure a direct return on investment.

The remuneration system consists of two elements: basic salary and performance-related bonuses. These bonuses take a variety of forms like monthly commission or a bonus/reward calculated monthly, quarterly, or yearly and on the basis of self-performance, team performance, or the firm's general outcomes. Nevertheless, it is common that all additives to basic salary are strictly related to the firm's financial outcomes. Such a mechanism is applied with regard to all employees regardless of the post they occupy. Only one company (**G**) claimed it diversifies the remuneration and reward system with regard to department and position.

In the investigated companies, there are no procedures which refer to the situation of dismissals or resignations. Such a situation stems mostly from the retention level. As previously mentioned, all companies declare they have a very low level of employee fluctuation. Two companies (**C** and **G**) have introduced some special activities which are undertaken in the case of the retirement of their employees.

The key employees' competences that were pointed out by respondents are fluency in a foreign language (mainly English), competences related to selling and customer care (in the case of salesforce), and technical competences (in the case of production employees). Additionally, high engagement and focus on the company were mentioned. Only one respondent claimed that the level of these competences among employees is moderate, while all others stated that it is high.

Based on the theoretical background and framework (Section 4.1) proposing that companies utilise various approaches to managing human resources in order to achieve their business goals, an attempt was made to examine that phenomenon in the described case studies. As a base for this analysis four configurations were adopted namely: commitment-based, collaboration-based, productivity-based, and compliance-based HRM. In all but one of the investigated companies, various architectures of the abovementioned approaches are used. Only in the case of Company C was a single approach declared and it was a commitment-based HRM, which focuses on competence development and maintaining a long-term employee commitment. It is an IT company providing software for monitoring production and the processing of orders. All employees are valued as equally important. In this place, is worth mentioning that the commitment-based configuration is a part of HRM practices architecture in five other companies (A, D, F, G, H).

The collaboration-based configuration which emphasises a special focus on building interpersonal relationships is a component of HRM architecture in most cases. Only in two companies (C and E) was that approach left out. Company C as an IT firm focuses mainly on personnel development, while Company E as a producer and seller of window joinery focuses mainly on productivity and emphasises compliance with defined standards to ensure the expected cost-effectiveness.

The productivity-based configuration which emphasises a person-job fit and focuses on achieving the expected performance is a part of HRM architecture in half of the conducted case studies. Three of these (D, G, and H) are companies which are characterised by complex HRM architecture consisting of all configurations, and one is Company E, in which HRM architecture includes two configurations, namely productivity-based and compliance-based.

The compliance-based configuration which emphasises compliance with defined standards, requirements, and other arrangements is utilised in most analysed cases. Besides the firms which adopt a mix of all configurations (D, G, and H), in one firm (F), the compliance-based configuration fits with two other configurations, namely commitment-based and collaboration-based HRM. Finally, Company E adopts an HRM architecture consisting of productivity-based and compliance-based configurations.

HRM architecture consisting of all four configurations occurs in three companies (D, G, and H). All these configurations constitute a mix which depends on such contingencies as the stage of company development or categories and the maturity of employees. All three companies apply this approach to all employees.

To sum up, it can be concluded that commitment-based, collaboration-based, and compliance-based configurations are most often (six times) components of HRM architecture in the analysed case studies while productivity-based configuration occurs four times.

After analysing the opinions of the respondents representing eight companies, depicted in the form of case studies in the previous subchapter, a general picture could be portrayed that all of them successfully managed their human resources. In most cases it is emphasised that goals are achieved and no real issues occur. Nevertheless, it is the respondent's opinion that there is always something to be improved (B, G). In one single company (E), the attraction and retention of production workers was reported as a challenge due to shortages on the labour market. In most of the companies, no changes or modifications in the field of HRM were reported. Only in one company (G) were new IT solutions in the field of HR administration implemented. In two other companies (E and H), the introduction of remote work was highlighted as an example of change in the HRM area.

In most of the companies, some innovations were implemented as consequence of business profile, market pressure, and other external constraints. Only in one single company (F) were no activities in that field reported within two last years. Among the implemented innovations were product innovations (A, B, D, and H), process innovations (B and C), and organisational innovations (E, G, and H).

Referring to the business outcomes, good financial standing and a stable market position of all companies have been identified. In general, despite some specificity of individual cases in terms of the dynamics of incomes, sale, market share, or cost optimisation, the overall situation was reported to be on the same level as in other companies in the industry (A, C, D, E, F, and H) or even better (B and G).

6 Conclusions

Conducted research showed both similarities and contradictions within the SMEs that operate internationally. According to the research model, HRM practices were the focal point in analyses, and these practices were strongly related with the context within which the investigated companies operate and the outcomes they achieve.

Our research confirmed the existence and impact of various contextual factors on the investigated companies. These companies varied with regard to business profile, age, the industry they operate in, and the potential occurrence of family relationships and ownership. The number of possible combinations of these factors presented the opportunity for every enterprise to be analysed individually. Nevertheless, limiting the scope of contextual factors only to those referring to the pace of internationalisation, business range and business profile, made it possible to create some commonalities that were presented in Chapter 5. On the basis of quantitative data which were substantiated by interviews, it can be concluded that external environmental factors are crucial in analysing the pace of internationalisation. Some of the investigated companies were oriented on international markets since their inception – in such cases, external contextual factors were perceived as enablers or obstacles in achieving the desired level of activity on foreign markets. Nevertheless, some of the SMEs were initially focused only on the domestic market, and their internationalisation started due to developed networks and business relationships as well as favourable circumstances. Such a situation mostly seems to concern late internationalisers. It can be concluded that the external context is crucial at the stage of making the decision whether or not to enter the foreign market in the case of mature organisations functioning on the domestic market for several years. In the case of such enterprises, the configuration of external factors can even be perceived as a trigger for internationalisation even though the

DOI: 10.4324/9781003319979-6

owner/founder might not have previously considered entering the foreign market.

The research was aimed at identifying HRM practices introduced in SMEs that began to operate internationally shortly after their establishment. Thus, our analysis was focused on the following issues: the level of structurisation of tasks and duties (especially those attributed to key employees), recruitment and selection, training and development, appraisal and remuneration. On the basis of the gathered data, the following findings can be presented.

In EIFs, the scope of duties of employees (especially those perceived to be of key importance) is precisely defined. Tasks match individual traits and create opportunities to make use of employees' potential. Moreover, key employees are frequently responsible for diverse tasks and multifunctional duties. Such a situation may stem from the fact that such organisations are quite young and their internal processes are not yet structured. These firms seek the optimal configuration of processes by modifying and developing them to meet the required performance level. Key employees are perceived as those who can link different activities and introduce innovative solutions.

In the staffing process, EIFs pay attention to candidates' potential and their prospective contribution to a firm's performance. These companies aim to choose the best candidate from the pool of those who applied for the job. During selection, EIFs focus strongly on evaluating teamwork, job-related knowledge and experience in the industry. Such an approach may reflect a willingness to acquire employees whose competences would fill a gap in industry-related knowledge and who would quickly assimilate with other employees.

EIFs are focused on conducting training and development programmes that aim to acquire appropriate and up-to-date knowledge referring to legal rules and regulations affecting a firm's functioning. Such programmes concentrate on obtaining competences that increase short-term performance.

With regard to the appraisal system, it focuses on the evaluation of work quality and employees' contribution to a firm's goals achievement. Additionally, in the evaluation process, objective and measurable criteria of performance are applied. These companies, relatively less frequently apply criteria that make it possible to appraise the compliance of employees' behaviour with a firm's rules, procedures, and standards. This may stem from the fact that in young companies, such rules and standards could not yet have been developed.

In EIF, the analyses of market wages are more frequently used to set the level of key employees' salaries. In such companies, individual bonuses and rewards are also quite common, and team rewards and long-term bonuses are seldom introduced.

Such findings are supported by information obtained during interviews conducted with representatives of eight companies. It should be stated that all activities introduced and undertaken are strongly focused on assuring the expected level of goal achievement and performance. Among all the processes run in these organisations, a relatively higher quality can be attributed to job structurisation, the monitoring of task fulfilment and the rewarding of performance. The investigated companies have precisely defined job descriptions which are not modified or changed. Outcomes are evaluated monthly, quarterly, or yearly. The results of the evaluation are used to define the level of rewards; and the development programmes are aimed at assuring the competences required for appropriate task fulfilment. However, it should be acknowledged on the basis of the cross-case analysis of HR processes that the level of their professionalisation and formalisation is rather low.

The analysis of quantitative and qualitative data enabled us to address the research questions posed in Chapter 4, which referred to defining the importance of HRM in EIFs; identifying the configurations of HRM practices used by EIFs and their outcomes; comparing them with late internationalised SMEs; analysing the differentiation of HRM configurations among EIFs with respect to their different trajectories in the post-entry phase; and determining how the challenges faced by these companies affect HRM.

Regarding the relevance of HRM in SMEs that internationalised early, our survey revealed two approaches occurring in this context with almost equal frequency. Thus, there is a small advantage of companies with HR strategies, while slightly less than half are those entities where such a strategy is absent. This 'duality', however, does not translate into substantial differences in the application of HRM practices. Interestingly, the average utilisation levels of the aforementioned practices were moderately high (between 66% and 82% of the maximum scale value), with the exception of the lower scores on remuneration practices. The respondents' evaluation of individual HRM practices indicates that, in general, more emphasis is placed on structuring work, supporting employees in achieving high performance, and employee retention.

It should be noted, however, that the utilisation level of a given practice only proves its presence and informs about prevalence but does not reflect its advancement or quality. Thus, in order to more thoroughly answer the first research question, the aforementioned findings should be supplemented with observations from qualitative study. In the case of the latter, we found that key employees are in general recognised as strategic assets, but this view is not usually associated with the development of formalised HR strategies, and HRM practices or services addressed to these employees. Furthermore, the appreciation of the importance of employees and the need of adequate management, declared by interviewees, rarely entailed a substantial change in terms of HRM professionalisation. In this respect, our conclusions are consistent with the features of HRM widely recognised in previous literature, such as flexibility, low formalisation, and the use of simplified practices in SMEs either operating in domestic markets or following an incremental path of internationalisation. Consistent with Glaister et al. (2014), the qualitative data demonstrated that for mature EIFs 'size matters' in respect to in-house HRM expertise. In the mid-sized entities, this expertise was embedded in the organisational unit accountable for ensuring an appropriate base of knowledge and competence resources, whereas smaller entities eagerly outsourced HR processes.

Regarding similarities between early and late internationalisers, we found no statistically significant differences in relation to HR strategy and the use of the core configurations of HRM practices. This may imply that enterprises that differ in terms of speed in the initial stages of internationalisation tend to converge in terms of organisational processes and practices during the advanced phase, which is in line with the typical scenario for mature EIFs suggested by Gabrielsson et al. (2008). Moreover, our findings suggest that in both groups, regardless of their internationalisation pattern, the same bundles of practices, namely commitment-based and collaboration-based, support firm innovation, which is consistent with a previous study by Zhou et al. (2013) in the Chinese context. Our study also revealed that in these two groups of internationalisers, the aforementioned configurations of HRM practice work differently in terms of their contribution to business performance by emphasising the relevance of the collaboration-based approach in EIFs, which is consistent with their particular reliance on networks and relationships reported in BG/INVs literature.

Based on prior studies, we expected that early internationalisers do not constitute a homogenous category of global market players, which was confirmed in this research. More specifically, three categories of such companies emerged, which varied in terms of international complexity and involvement in foreign markets. Their common attributes included a relatively lower level of remuneration practices and the use of all HRM configurations without a predominant approach. In the case of the latter feature, similar conclusions can be drawn from qualitative research, where commitment, collaboration, and compliance approaches coexisted in as many as six out of eight cases. It can therefore be concluded that such a 'combinative' practice is a kind of golden mean in the conditions of complexity and turbulence of the environment as well as the needs of efficiency and effectiveness specific to firms with greater international experience. As regards the international experience of EIFs participating in the qualitative study, it is worth recalling that almost all of them started that they were operating in foreign markets almost immediately after their inception, thus their transition to an internationalised company did not entail any substantial changes in HRM, except from the greater emphasis on developing foreign language skills by employees.

Regarding the differences in HRM among EIFs, SMEs operating as European exporters turned out to be significantly less advanced compared to the companies characterised by greater exposure to international complexity (i.e. global exporters) or multifaceted involvement in overseas activities (i.e. by non-equity and equity entry modes). This applies to both the strategic importance and the utilisation level of most HRM practices, with the exception of the compliance-based bundle. Additionally, our study revealed that EIFs that operate globally adopted an idiosyncratic pattern of combining the core configurations. More specifically, compared to other companies, they put more emphasis on collaboration-, commitment-, and productivity-based sets of practices that are aimed at ensuring unique and strategically valuable human capital (Lepak & Snell, 2002).

In addition to the challenges arising from international complexity and the differentiation of international activities, most of the investigated companies cope successfully with COVID-related constraints and consequences such higher absenteeism or supply chain collapse. Apart from the aforementioned contingencies, EIFs constantly had to adjust to other changes in their external environment concerning customers' expectations and technology, and more rarely, stemming from fierce global competition. However, according to almost all interviewees, these adjustments are now rather incremental than radical, although the perceived pace of external changes seems greater than in the initial phase of their business activity. Therefore, balancing needs of greater performance and sufficient flexibility remains an unavoidable necessity for managing human resources in these entities, whereas employee features, regarded as key success factors in times of environmental volatility, uncertainty, and crisis (e.g.

caused by the pandemic), include their professional/technical knowledge, skills, flexibility, and commitment.

On the basis of conducted research, the following conclusions regarding early internationalised SMEs can be drawn:

- The owner/CEO plays the principal role in effective people management. In almost all cases, they are highlighted as a person who coordinates HR-related activities.
- The importance of employees (their competences and commitment) is emphasised in these organisations. It mostly refers to key employees but such a specific group of workers is seldom identified in these companies. In most cases, all the hired staff are perceived to be important in assuring a firms' performance.
- HRM is an ongoing activity which is executed in accordance with emerging needs and no strategic/long-term plans are developed and executed.
- Tasks referring to HR are covered by an HR department or a single post, external HR services providers or in a mixed model according to which some tasks are executed by internal HR employees and some are outsourced. The factors that impact upon the decision about the approach to be chosen are industry, firm's size, and the attitude of the manager/owner to HR.
- The emergence on international markets was not associated with any changes in HR activities. Respondents claimed that employees were well prepared to perform tasks and that both the way HR processes were developed and the way they are executed is sufficient and requires no modifications.
- These companies have stable and cooperating staff. All companies claimed that they seldom recruit new employees, and if they do so, it is mainly because of employee retirement or periodic increases in the sales level rather than through resignations. Having a very high retention level may also stem from paying attention to engagement and perceiving '*focus on the company*' as a key employees' competence.
- Employees' knowledge, skills, and commitment were pointed out as a key factor in coping with difficulties stemming from shocks and crises (e.g. COVID-19).

Our research confirmed that in the investigated companies HRM processes are simplified and it is an owner or CEO who plays a crucial role in the design of employee-related activities – such findings are in line with general view of HRM in SMEs. Additionally, employees have great common sense and feel they are a part of the organisation, which was also discussed in scientific literature.

However, what seems to differentiate internationally active SMEs (especially EIFs) from others is a strong focus on performance, which is reflected in the following: (1) precisely defined and seldom modified scope of tasks for job positions; (2) acquiring employees who can potentially contribute to firms' long-term goals; (3) hiring candidates with a high level of industry-specific knowledge; (4) organising training aimed at the development of competences required for appropriate task fulfilment or providing employees with actual knowledge about legal acts and regulations; (5) concentrating on individual performance and achievements during appraisals; (6) introducing performance-related individual rewards and bonuses. The combination of the aforementioned practices seems to describe the general approach to HRM in companies operating on international markets. Additionally, such an approach assures performance as the vast majority of the investigated companies claimed to achieve an increase in income in the 2018–2019 period, and they additionally confirmed the introduction of process or product/service innovations.

Our results also confirmed that HRM practices introduced and executed in internationally active SMEs are not comparable to those existing in MNEs. Such a situation stems mostly from the lack of HR departments or HR-related job positions and the lack of expertise that would help in designing and introducing advanced HRM processes.

Based on a previous literature analysis and conducted research, some implications for practice can be drawn. To begin with, SMEs decision-makers' awareness and HRM knowledge are crucial for the design of people management practices in EIFs. Thus, it is important to provide owners and managers with an opportunity to obtain HR-related knowledge, develop their skills, and build appropriate attitudes. This can be obtained by training and development programmes, by setting cooperation with HR consultants or by hiring HR specialists who will develop and introduce a firm's specific HR processes. As in many investigated organisations, line managers were in charge of HR-related issues, training and development programmes aimed at team management or HRM practices should also be offered to them. In addition, social climate and employees' relationships seem to be crucial in assuring performance and employees' commitment. Thus, owners/managers should pay attention to building 'team spirit' as it can be an important issue which supports HRM. Next, employees should be provided with training enabling the development of such competences as relationship building and teamwork as well as the possibility to attend courses increasing fluency in foreign languages. Finally, despite the fact that such an issue was seldom mentioned by respondents, the development of cross-cultural competences seems to be an emerging need while intensifying international activity. For now, most owners and managers may not be aware that higher engagement in operations on foreign markets may require preparedness with regard to cultural differences. The aforementioned implications are addressed to owners/ managers of SMEs, but such proposals should also be the concern of institutions aimed at supporting SMEs in their international activity.

Our empirical study has some limitations. In the case of the quantitative research, they stem from the cross-sectional nature, homogeneity of companies in terms of country of origin (Poland), and the forms of international activity (exporting and foreign direct investments), which limit the generalisability of the findings. Another important aspect refers to COVID-related contingencies that constrained the availability of potential respondents. Regardless of the measures taken to control the direct impact of the pandemic on HRM, the possibility of more complex, indirect effects on the obtained data cannot be fully excluded. Thus, to validate our findings and enhance their applicability, we suggest further quantitative research that also covers other institutional contexts and collaboration entry modes used by SMEs within the accelerated internationalisation. Regarding the qualitative study, it should be emphasised that initially, we planned to conduct interviews with direct, personal contact at the premises of selected companies. This approach would have also provided an opportunity for using other methods of collecting data (e.g. observation and informal interviews). Unfortunately, the aforementioned strategy could not be implemented due to the pandemic situation, which hindered direct access to selected interviewees and other sources of empirical data. As we had to adopt a strategy that would both ensure the equivalence of the research context and address the concerns of the participants of this study, we applied a unified, yet less 'fruitful' solution, that is, webcam interviews with decision-makers. Therefore, we believe that further qualitative studies should complement our findings with other points of view (e.g. those of individual core employees directly involved in international activities), and sources of data, such as direct observation and internal documents.

References

Ahokangas, P., Juho, A., & Haapanen, L. (2010). Toward the theory of temporary competitive advantage in internationalization. In R. Sanchez & A. Heene (Eds.), *Enhancing competences for competitive advantage* (pp. 121–144). Bingley: Emerald Group Publishing Limited. doi: 10.1108/S0749-6826(2010)0000012008

Almor, T., & Hashai, N. (2004). The competitive advantage and strategic configuration of knowledge-intensive, small-and medium-sized multinationals: A modified resource-based view. *Journal of International Management, 10*(4), 479–500. doi: 10.1016/j.intman.2004.08.002

Almor, T., Tarba, S. Y., & Margalit, A. (2014). Maturing, technology-based, Born-Global companies: Surviving through mergers and acquisitions. *Management International Review, 54*, 421–444. doi: 10.1007/s11575-014-0212-9

Anderson, E., & Gatignon, H. (1986). Modes of foreign entry: A transaction cost analysis and propositions. *Journal of International Business Studies, 17*, 1–26. doi: 10.1057/palgrave.jibs.8490432

Aspelund, A., Madsen, T. K., & Moen, Ø. (2007). A review of the foundation, international marketing strategies, and performance of international new ventures. *European Journal of Marketing, 41*(11/12), 1423–1448. doi: 10.1108/03090560710821242

Ates, A., Garengo , P., Cocca, P., & Bititci, U. (2013). The development of SME managerial practice for effective performance management. *Journal of Small Business and Enterprise Development, 20*(1), pp. 28–54.

Attig, N., Boubakri, N., El Ghoul, S., & Guedhami, O. (2016). Firm internationalization and corporate social responsibility. *Journal of Business Ethics, 134*(2), 171–197. doi: 10.1007/s10551-014-2410-6

Autio, E., Sapienza, H. J., & Almeida, J. G. (2000). Effects of age at entry, knowledge intensity, and imitability on international growth. *Academy of Management Journal, 43*(5), 909–924. doi: 10.5465/1556419

Ayal, I., & Zif, J. (1979). Marketing expansion strategies in multinational marketing. *Journal of Marketing, 43*, 84–94. doi: 10.2307/1250744

Ayuso, S., & Navarrete-Baez, F. E. (2018). How does entrepreneurial and international orientation influence SMEs' commitment to sustainable development? Empirical evidence from Spain and Mexico. *Corporate Social Responsibility and Environmental Management, 25*(1), 80–94. doi:10.1002/csr.1441

Bannò, M., & Sgobbi, F. (2016). Family business characteristics and the approach to HRM in overseas ventures. *Journal of Small Business Management, 54*(2), 640–658. doi:10.1111/jsbm.12162

Baum, M., Schwens, C., Kabst, R. (2014). Determinants of different types of born globals. In M. Gabrielsson & V. H. M. Kirpalani (Eds.), *Handbook of research on born globals* (pp. 36–45). Cheltenham: Edward Elgar Publishing Ltd.

Baum, M., Schwens, C., & Kabst, R. (2015). A latent class analysis of small firms' internationalization patterns. *Journal of World Business, 50*(4), 754–768. doi:10.1016/j.jwb.2015.03.001

Bell, J., Crick, D., & Young, S. (2004). Small firm internationalization and business strategy: An exploratory study of 'knowledge-intensive' and 'traditional' manufacturing firms in the UK. *International Small Business Journal, 22*(1), 23–56. doi:10.1177/0266242604039479

Bell, J., McNaughton, R., & Young, S. (2001). Born-again global' firms: An extension to the 'born global' phenomenon. *Journal of International Management, 7*(3), 173–189. doi:10.1016/S1075-4253(01)00043-6

Bell, J., McNaughton, R., Young, S., & Crick, D. (2003). Towards an integrative model of small firm internationalisation. *Journal of International Entrepreneurship, 1*(4), 339–362. doi:10.1023/A:1025629424041

Bell, R. G., Filatotchev, I., & Rasheed, A. A. (2012). The liability of foreignness in capital markets: Sources and remedies. *Journal of International Business Studies, 43*(2), 107–122. doi:10.1057/jibs.2011.55

Bennett, N., & Lemoine, G. J. (2014). What a difference a word makes: Understanding threats to performance in a VUCA world. *Business Horizons, 57*(3), 311–317. doi:10.1016/j.bushor.2014.01.001

Berber, N., Morley, M. J., Slavić, A., & Poór, J. (2017). Management compensation systems in Central and Eastern Europe: A comparative analysis. *The International Journal of Human Resource Management, 28*(2), 1661–1689. doi:10.1080/09585192.2016.1277364

Bilkey, W. J., & Tesar, G. (1977). The export behavior of smaller-sized Wisconsin manufacturing firms. *Journal of International Business Studies, 8*(1), 93–98. doi:10.1057/palgrave.jibs.8490783

Boocock, G., & Anderson, V. (2003). International business and UK SMEs: Rationale, routes, readiness, role of government support, and reflections. *The International Journal of Entrepreneurship and Innovation, 4*(2), 97–111. doi:10.5367/000000003101299456

Breuillot, A. (2021). Exploring the role of diversity management during early internationalizing firms' internationalization process. *Management International Review, 61*, 125–156. doi:10.1007/s11575-021-00440-3

Brewer, P. (2007). Operationalizing psychic distance: A revised approach. *Journal of International Marketing, 15*(1), 44–66. doi:10.1509/jimk.15.1.004

Brewster, C., & Mayrhofer, W. (Eds.) (2012). *Handbook of research on comparative human resource management.* Cheltenham, UK; Northampton, MA: Edward Elgar Publishing.

Brewster, C., Mayrhofer, W., & Farndale, E. (Eds.) (2018). *Handbook of research on comparative human resource management* (2nd ed.). Cheltenham, UK; Northampton, MA: Edward Elgar Publishing.

Brewster, C., Smale, A., & Mayrhofer, W. (2017). Globalisation and human resource management. In P. Sparrow & S. C. L. Cooper (Eds.), *A research agenda for human resource management* (pp. 201–218). Cheltenham, UK; Northampton, MA: Edward Elgar Publishing.

Briscoe, R., Schuler, R., & Claus, L. (2009). *International human resource management. Policies and practices for multinational enterprises* (3rd ed.). New York and London: Routledge.

Brislin, R. W. (1970). Back-translation for cross-cultural research. *Journal of Cross-Cultural Psychology, 1*(3), 185–216. doi:10.1177/135910457000100301

Bruneel, J., & De Cock, R. (2016). Entry mode research and SMEs: A review and future research agenda. *Journal of Small Business Management, 54*(sup1), 135–167. doi:10.1111/jsbm.12291

Buckley, P. J., & Casson, M. A. (1999). Theory of international operations. In P. J. Buckley & P. Ghauri (Eds.), *The internationalisation of the firm: A reader* (pp. 55–60). London: Academic Press.

Buzavaite, M., & Korsakiene, R. (2019). Human capital and the internationalisation of SMEs: A systemic literature review. *Entrepreneurial Business and Economics Review, 7*(3), 125–142. doi:10.15678/EBER.2019.070307

Calof J. L., & Beamish, P. W. (1995). Adapting to foreign markets: Explaining internationalization. *International Business Review, 4*(2), 115–131. doi:10.1016/0969-5931(95)00001-G

Cannone, G., & Ughetto, E. (2014). Born globals: A cross-country survey on high-tech start-ups. *International Business Review, 23*(1), 272–283. doi:10.1016/j.ibusrev.2013.05.003

Cavusgil, S. T. (1980). On the internationalization process of firms. *European Research, 8*(6), 273–281.

Cesinger, B., Fink, M., Madsen, T. K., & Kraus, S. (2012). Rapidly internationalizing ventures: How definitions can bridge the gap across contexts. *Management Decision, 50*(10), 1816–1842. doi:10.1108/00251741211279620

Chandra, A., Paul, J., & Chavan, M. (2020). Internationalization barriers of SMEs from developing countries: A review and research agenda. *International Journal of Entrepreneurial Behavior & Research, 26*(6), 1281–1310. doi:10.1108/IJEBR-03-2020-0167

Chandra, Y., Styles, C., & Wilkinson, I. F. (2012). An opportunity-based view of rapid internationalization. *Journal of International Marketing, 20*(1), 74–102. doi:10.1509/jim.10.0147

Chang, S.-J., & Rhee, J. H. (2011). Rapid FDI expansion and firm performance. *Journal of International Business Studies, 42*(8), 979–994. doi: 10.105 7/jibs.2011.30

Cheng, H. L., & Yu, C. M. J. (2008). Institutional pressures and initiation of internationalization: Evidence from Taiwanese small-and medium-sized enterprises. *International Business Review, 17*(3), 331–348. doi: 10.1016/ j.ibusrev.2008.01.006

Chetty, S., & Campbell-Hunt, C. (2004). A strategic approach to internationalization: A tradition versus a "born global" approach. *Journal of International Marketing, 12*(1), 57–81. doi: 10.1509/jimk.12.1.57.25651

Chetty, S., Johanson, M., & Martín Martín, O. (2014). Speed of internationalization: Conceptualization, measurement and validation. *Journal of World Business, 49*(4), 633–650. doi: 10.1016/j.jwb.2013.12.014

Chi, N.-W., Wu, C.-Y., & Lin, C. Y.-Y. (2008). Does training facilitate SME's performance? *The International Journal of Human Resource Management, 19*(10), 1962–1975. doi: 10.1080/09585190802324346

Child, J., Karmowska, J., & Shenkar, O. (2022). The role of context in SME internationalization – A review. *Journal of World Business, 57*(1), 101267. doi: 10.1016/j.jwb.2021.101267

Ciszewska-Mlinarič, M., Wójcik, P., & Obłój, K. (2020). Learning dynamics of rapidly internationalizing venture: Beyond the early stage of international growth in a CEE context. *Journal of Business Research, 108*, 450–465. doi: 1 0.1016/j.jbusres.2019.03.002

Clark, D. R., Li, D., & Shepherd, D. A. (2018). Country familiarity in the initial stage of foreign market selection. *Journal of International Business Studies, 49*, 442–472. doi: 10.1057/s41267-017-0099-3

Contractor, F. J., Hsu, C. -C., & Kundu, S. K. (2005). Explaining export performance: A comparative study of international new ventures in Indian and Taiwanese Software Industry. *Management International Review, 45*(S3), 83–110. http://www.jstor.org/stable/40836144

Cooke, F. L. (2018). Concepts, contexts, and mindsets: Putting human resource management research in perspectives. *Human Resource Management Journal, 28*, 1–13. doi: 10.1111/1748-8583.12163

Cortellazzo, L., Bonesso, S., & Gerli, F. (2020). Entrepreneurs' behavioural competencies for internationalisation: Exploratory insights from the Italian context. *International Journal of Entrepreneurial Behaviour and Research, 26*(4), 723–747. doi: 10.1108/IJEBR-12-2018-0806

Coviello, N. E., & McAuley, A. (1999). Internationalisation and the smaller firm: A review of contemporary empirical research. *Management International Review, 39*(3), 223–256. http://www.jstor.org/stable/40835788

Cranet. (2017). *International executive report 2017, Cranet survey on comparative human resource management.* Cranfield: Cranet-Cranfield University.

Cyert, R. M., & March, J. G. (1963). *A behavioral theory of the firm.* Englewood Cliffs, NJ: Prentice-Hall.

Dana, L. P. (2001). Introduction: Networks, internationalization, and policy. *Small Business Economics, 16*(2), 57–62. doi: 10.1023/A:1011199116576

D'Angelo, A., Majocchi, A., & Buck, T. (2016). External managers, family ownership and the scope of SME internationalization. *Journal of World Business, 51*(4), 534–547. doi: 10.1016/j.jwb.2016.01.004

D'Angelo, A., Majocchi, A., Zucchella, A., & Buck, T. (2013). Geographical pathways for SME internationalization: Insights from an Italian sample. *International Marketing Review, 30*(2), 80–105. doi: 10.1108/02651331311314538

Daszkiewicz, N., & Wach, K. (2013). *Małe i średnie przedsiębiorstwa na rynkach międzynarodowych*. Kraków: Wydawnictwo UEK.

De Clercq, D., Sapienza, H. J., & Crijns, H. (2005). The internationalization of small and medium-sized firms. *Small Business Economics, 24*(4), 409–419. doi: 10.1007/s11187-005-5333-x

De Clercq, D., Sapienza, H. J., Yavuz, R. I., & Zhou, L. (2012). Learning and knowledge in early internationalization research: Past accomplishments and future directions. *Journal of Business Venturing, 27*, 143–165. doi: 10.1016/j.jbusvent.2011.09.003

Deligianni, I., Voudouris, I., & Lioukas, S. (2015). Growth paths of small technology firms: The effect of different knowledge type over time. *Journal of World Business, 50*, 491–504. doi: 10.1016/j.jwb.2014.08.006

Dickmann, M., Brewster, C., & Sparrow P. (Eds.) (2016). *International human resource management. Contemporary human resource issues in Europe*. Routledge.

Dominguez, N., & Mayrhofer, U. (2017). Internationalization stages of traditional SMEs: Increasing, decreasing and re-increasing commitment to foreign markets. *International Business Review, 26*, 1051–1063. doi: 10.1016/j.ibusrev.2017.03.010

Donaldson, L. (2001). *The contingency theory of organizations*. Thousand Oaks/London/New Delhi: Sage.

Dowling, P. J., Festing, M., Engle, A. D. (2008). *International human resource management* (5th ed.). London: Thomson Learning.

Dzikowski, P. (2018). A bibliometric analysis of born global firms. *Journal of Business Research, 85*, 281–294. doi: 10.1016/j.jbusres.2017.12.054

Edwards, T. (2015). The transfer of employment practices across borders in multinational companies. In A. W. Harzing & A. H. Pinnington (Eds.), *International human resource management* (4th ed., pp. 80–105). Los Angeles, et al.: Sage.

Efrat, K., & Shoham, A. (2012). Born global firms: The differences between their short- and long-term performance drivers. *Journal of World Business, 47*, 675–685. doi: 10.1016/j.jwb.2012.01.015

Eisenhardt, K., & Graebner, M. (2007). Theory building from cases: Opportunities and challenges. *Academy of Management Journal, 50*(1), 25–32. doi: 10.5465/amj.2007.24160888

Eisenhardt, K. M., & Martin, J. A. (2000). Dynamic capabilities: What are they?. *Strategic Management Journal, 21*, 1105–1121. doi: 10.1002/1097-0266(200010/11)21:10/11<1105::AID-SMJ133>3.0.CO;2-E

European Commission. (2010). *Internationalisation of European SMEs – Final report*. Brussels: European Commission. https://wbc-rti.info/object/document/7933/attach/internationalisation_sme_final_en.pdf

European Commission. (2017). *Annual report on European SMEs 2016/17*. doi:10.2873/742338

European Commission. (2020). *An SME strategy for a sustainable and digital Europe*. Communication from the Commission to the European Parliament, the Council, the European Economic and Social Committee and the Committee of the Regions. https://eur-lex.europa.eu/legal-content/EN/TXT/PDF/?uri=CELEX:52020DC0103&from=EN (accessed 18 July 2022).

Eurostat. (2021). *SMEs weight in EU's international trade in goods*. https://ec.europa.eu/eurostat/web/products-eurostat-news/-/ddn-20211006-2 (accessed 18 July 2022).

Ferguson, S., Henrekson, M., & Johannesson, L. (2021). Getting the facts right on born globals. *Small Business Economy, 56*, 259–276. doi:10.1007/s11187-019-00216-y

Fernandez, Z., & Nieto, M. J. (2006). Impact of ownership on the international involvement of SMEs. *Journal of International Business Studies, 37*, 340–351. doi:10.1057/palgrave.jibs.8400196

Fernhaber, S. A., & Li, D. (2013). International exposure through network relationships: Implications for new venture internationalization. *Journal of Business Venturing, 28*, 316–334. doi:10.1016/j.jbusvent.2012.05.002

Festing, M., Harsch, K., Schaefer, L., Scullion, H. (2017). Talent management in small- and medium-sized enterprises. In D. G. Collings, K. Mellahi, & W. F. Cascio (Eds.), *The Oxford handbook of talent management* (pp. 478–493). Oxford: Oxford University Press.

Festing, M., Schäfer, L., & Scullion, H. (2013). Talent management in medium-sized German companies: an explorative study and agenda for future research. *The International Journal of Human Resource Management, 24*(9), 1872–1893.

Finstad, K. (2010). Response interpolation and scale sensitivity: Evidence against 5-point scales. *Journal of Usability Studies, 5*(3), 104–110. https://dl.acm.org/doi/abs/10.5555/2835434.2835437

Francioni, B., Pagano, A., & Castellani, D. (2016). Drivers of SMEs' exporting activity: A review and a research agenda. *Multinational Business Review, 24*(3), 194–215. doi:10.1108/MBR-06-2016-0023

Freeman, S. (2014). Born global firms' use of networks and alliances: A social dynamic perspective. In M. Gabrielsson & V. H. M. Kirpalani (Eds.), *Handbook of research on born globals* (pp. 128–144). Cheltenham: Edward Elgar Publishing Ltd.

Freeman, S., Edwards, R., & Schroder, B. (2006). How smaller born-global firms use networks and alliances to overcome constraints to rapid internationalization. *Journal of International Marketing, 14*(3), 33–63. doi:10.1509/jimk.14.3.33

Freeman, S., Hutchings, K., Lazaris, M., & Zyngier, S. (2010). A model of rapid knowledge development: The smaller born-global firm. *International Business Review, 19*(1), 70–84. doi:10.1016/j.ibusrev.2009.09.004

Freixanet, J., & Renart, G. (2020). A capabilities perspective on the joint effects of internationalization time, speed, geographic scope and managers' competencies on SME survival. *Journal of World Business*, *55*(6), 101110. doi: 10.1016/j.jwb.2020.101110

Gabrielsson, M., Gabrielsson, P., & Dimitratos, P. (2014). International entrepreneurial culture and growth of international new ventures. *Management International Review*, *54*(4), 445–471. doi: 10.1007/s11575-014-0213-8

Gabrielsson, M., & Kirpalani, V. H. M. (2004). Born globals: How to reach new business space rapidly. *International Business Review*, *13*(5), 555–571. doi: 10.1016/j.ibusrev.2004.03.005

Gabrielsson, M., Kirpalani, V. H. M., Dimitratos, P., Solberg, C. A., & Zucchella, A. (2008). Born globals: Propositions to help advance the theory. *International Business Review*, *17*(4), 385–401. doi: 10.1016/j.ibusrev.2008.02.015

Gabrielsson, P., & Gabrielsson, M. (2013). A dynamic model of growth phases and survival in international business-to-business new ventures: The moderating effect of decision-making logic. *Industrial Marketing Management*, *42*(8), 1357–1373. doi: 10.106/j.indmarman.2013.07.011

Ganitsky, J. (1989). Strategies for innate and adoptive exporters: Lessons from Israel's case. *International Marketing Review*, *6*(5), 50–65. doi: 10.1108/EUM0000000001523

García-García, R., García-Canal, E., & Guillén, M. F. (2017). Rapid internationalization and long-term performance: The knowledge link. *Journal of World Business*, *52*, 97–110. doi: 10.1016/j.jwb.2016.09.005

Glaister, A. J., Liu, Y., Sahadev, S., & Gomes, E. (2014). Externalizing, internalizing and fostering commitment: The case of born-global firms in emerging economies. *Management International Review*, *54*, 473–496. doi: 10.1007/s11575-014-0215-6

Grant, R. M. (1991). The resource-based theory of competitive advantage: Implications for strategy formulation. *California Management Review*, *33*(3), 114–135. doi: 10.2307/41166664

Gruenhagen, J. H., Gordon, S. R., Sawang, S., & Davidsson, P. (2018). International experience, growth aspirations, and internationalization of new ventures. *Journal of Entrepreneurship*, *16*, 421–440. doi: 10.1007/s10843-018-0232-9

Gulanowski, D., Papadopoulos, N., & Plante, L. (2018). The role of knowledge in international expansion. Toward an integration of competing models of internationalization. *Review of International Business and Strategy*, *28*(1), 35–60 doi: 10.1108/RIBS-09-2017-0077

Hagen, B., & Zucchella, A. (2014). Born global or born to run? The long-term growth of born global firms. *Management International Review*, *54*, 497–525. doi: 10.1007/s11575-014-0214-7

Hansen, N. K., Güttel, W. H., & Swart, J. (2019). HRM in dynamic environments: Exploitative, exploratory, and ambidextrous HR architectures. *The International Journal of Human Resource Management*, *30*(4), 648–679. doi: 10.1080/09585192.2016.1270985

Harney, B. (2021). Accommodating HRM in small and medium-sized enterprises (SMEs): A critical review. *Economic and Business Review, 23*(2). doi:10.15458/2335-4216.1007

Harney, B., & Alkhalaf, H. (2020). A quarter-century review of HRM in small and medium-sized enterprises: Capturing what we know, exploring where we need to go. *Human Resource Management*, 1–25. doi:10.1002/hrm.22010

Harzing, A. W., & Pinnington, A. H. (Eds.) (2015). *International Human Resource Management* (4th ed.). Los Angeles, et al.: Sage.

Heenan, D. A., & Perlmutter, H. V. (1979). *Multinational organization development*. Reading, MA: Addison-Wesley.

Heilmann, P., Forsten-Astikainen, R., & Kultalahti, S. (2020). Agile HRM practices of SMEs. *Journal of Small Business Management, 58*, 1291–1306. doi:10.1111/jsbm.12483

Hennart, J. F. (2014). The accidental internationalists: A theory of born globals. *Entrepreneurship Theory and Practice, 38*(1), 117–135. doi:10.1111/etap.12076

Hennart, J.-F., Majocchi, A., & Forlani, E. (2019). The myth of the stay-at-home family firm: How family-managed SMEs can overcome their internationalization limitations. *Journal of International Business Studies, 50*(5), 758–782. doi:10.1057/s41267-017-0091-y

Hernandez, M. A. (2019). Unveiling international new ventures' success: Employee's entrepreneurial behavior. *Administrative Sciences, 9*(3), 56. doi:10.3390/admsci9030056

Hilmersson, M., & Johanson, M. (2020). Knowledge acquisition strategy, speed of capability development and speed of SME internationalisation. *International Small Business Journal, 38*(6), 536–556. doi:10.1177/0266242620909029

Hilmersson, M., Johanson, M., Lundberg, H., & Papaioannou, S. (2017). Time, temporality, and internationalization: The relationship among point in time of, time to, and speed of international expansion. *Journal of International Marketing, 25*(1), 22–45. doi:10.1509/jim.16.0013

Hsu, W.-T., Chen, H.-L., & Cheng, C.-Y. (2013). Internationalization and firm performance of SMEs: The moderating effects of CEO attributes. *Journal of World Business, 48*, 1–12. doi:10.1016/j.jwb.2012.06.001

Hymer, S. H. (1960/1976). *The international operations of national firms: A study of direct foreign investment*. Cambridge, MA: MIT Press.

Inkpen, A. C. (2005). Strategic alliances. In M. A. Hitt, R. E. Freeman, & J. S. Harrison (Eds.), *The Blackwell handbook of strategic management* (pp. 403–427). Oxford, UK: Blackwell Publishers Ltd. doi:10.1111/b.9780631218616.2006.00015.x

Isidor, R., Schwens, C., & Kabst, R. (2011). Human resource management and early internationalization: Is there a leap-frogging in international staffing?. *The International Journal of Human Resource Management, 22*(10), 2167–2184, doi:10.1080/09585192.2011.580186

Jackson, S. E., & Schuler, R. S. (1995). Understanding human resource management in the context of organizations and their environments. *Annual Review of Psychology, 46*, 237–264. doi:10.1146/annurev.ps.46.020195.001321

Jiang, G., Kotabe, M., Zhang, F., Hao, A. W., Paul, J., & Wang, C. L. (2020). The determinants and performance of early internationalizing firms: A literature review and research agenda. *International Business Review, 29*(4), doi:10.1016/j.ibusrev.2019.101662

Johanson, J., & Mattson, L. G. (1987). Interorganizational relations in industrial systems—A network approach compared with the transaction cost approach. *International Studies of Management and Organization, 17*(1), 34–48. doi:10.1080/00208825.1987.11656444

Johanson, J., & Mattson, L. G. (2012). International marketing and internationalisation processes. A network approach. In P. W. Turnbull & S. J. Paliwoda (Eds.), *Research in international marketing* (pp. 234–265). London/ New York: Routledge.

Johanson, J., & Vahlne, J. E. (1977). The internationalization process of the firm: A model of knowledge development and increasing foreign market commitments. *Journal of International Business Studies, 8*(1), 23–32. doi:10. 1057/palgrave.jibs.8490676

Johanson, J., & Vahlne, J. E. (1990). The mechanism of internationalisation. *International Marketing Review, 7*(4), 11–24. doi:10.1108/0265133901013 7414

Johanson, J., & Vahlne, J. E. (2009). Uppsala internationalization process model revisited: From liability of foreignness to liability of outsidership. *Journal of International Business Studies, 40*(9), 1411–1431. doi:10.1057/ jibs.2009.24

Johanson, M., & Kalinic, I. (2016). Acceleration and deceleration in the internationalization process of the firm. *Management International Review, 56*, 827–847. doi:10.1007/s11575-016-0304-9

Johanson, M., & Martín Martín, O. (2015). The incremental expansion of Born Internationals: A comparison of new and old Born Internationals. *International Business Review, 24*, 476–496. doi:10.1016/j.ibusrev.2014. 10.006

Jones, M. V., & Coviello, N. E. (2005). Internationalisation: Conceptualizing and entrepreneurial process of behaviour in time. *Journal of International Business Studies, 36*(3), 284–303. doi:10.1057/palgrave.jibs.8400138

Jones, M. V., Coviello, N., & Tang, Y. K. (2011). International entrepreneurship research (1989–2009): A domain ontology and thematic analysis. *Journal of Business Venturing, 26*(6), 632–659. doi:10.1016/j.jbusvent.2011.04.001

Jones, M. V., & Young, S. (2009). Does entry mode matter? Reviewing current themes and perspectives. In M. V. Jones, P. Dimitratos, M. Fletcher, & S. Young (Eds.), *Internationalization, entrepreneurship and the smaller firm: Evidence from around the world* (pp. 6–19). Cheltenham/Northhampton: Edward Elgar Publishing.

Ketkar, S., & Sett, P. K. (2010). Environmental dynamism, human resource flexibility, and firm performance: Analysis of a multi-level causal model. *The International Journal of Human Resource Management, 21*(8), 1173–1206. doi:10.1080/09585192.2010.483841

Klein, S., & Roth, V. J.(1990). Determinants of export channel structure: The effects of experience and psychic distance reconsidered. *International Marketing Review*, 7(5), 27–38. doi:10.1108/EUM0000000001533

Knight, G. A., & Cavusgil, S. T. (1996). The born global firm: A challenge to traditional internationalization theory. In S. T. Cavusgil & T. Madsen (Eds.), *Advances in international marketing* (Vol. 8, pp. 11–26). Greenwich, CT: JAI Press.

Knight, G. A., & Cavusgil, S. T. (2004). Innovation, organizational capabilities, and the born-global firm. *Journal of International Business Studies*, 35(2), 124–141. doi:10.1057/palgrave.jibs.8400071

Knight, G. A., & Liesch, P. W. (2016). Internationalization: From incremental to born global. *Journal of World Business*, 51(1), 93–102. doi:10.1016/j.jwb.2015.08.011

Krishnan, T. N., & Scullion, H. (2017). Talent management and dynamic view of talent in small and medium enterprises. *Human Resource Management Review*, 27(3), 431–441.

Kuivalainen, O., Sundqvist, S., Saarenketo, S., & McNaughton, R. (2012). Internationalization patterns of small and medium-sized enterprises. *International Marketing Review*, 29(5), 448–465. doi:10.1108/02651331211260331

Kuivalainen, O., Sundqvist, S., & Servais, P. (2007). Firms' degree of born-globalness, international entrepreneurial orientation and export performance. *Journal of World Business*, 42, 253–267. doi:10.1016/j.jwb.2007.04.010

Kundu, S. K., & Katz, J. A. (2003). Born-International SMEs: BI-level impacts of resources and intentions. *Small Business Economics*, 20, 25–47. doi:10.1023/A:1020292320170

Lavie D., Stettner D., & Tushman, M. L. (2010). Exploration and exploitation within and across organizations. *The Academy of Management Annals*, 4(1), 109–155. doi:10.5465/19416521003691287

Lazaris, M., & Freeman, S. (2018). An examination of global mindset and international market opportunities among SMEs. *International Studies of Management, & Organization*, 48(2), 181–203. doi:10.1080/00208825.2018.1443739

Leonidou, L. C., Katsikeas, C. S., Palihawadana, D., & Spyropoulou, S. (2007). An analytical review of the factors stimulating smaller firms to export: Implications for policy-makers. *International Marketing Review*, 24(6), 735–770. doi:10.1108/02651330710832685

Lepak, D. P., & Snell, S. A. (1999). The human resource architecture: Toward a theory of human capital allocation and development. *The Academy of Management Review*, 24(1), 31–48. doi:10.5465/amr.1999.1580439

Lepak, D. P., & Snell, S. A. (2002). Examining the human resource architecture: The relationships among human capital, employment, and human resource configurations. *Journal of Management*, 28(4), 517–543. doi:10.1177/014920630202800403

Lepak, D. P., Takeuchi, R., & Snell, S. A. (2003). Employment flexibility and firm performance: Examining the interaction effects of employment mode, environmental dynamism, and technological intensity. *Journal of Management, 29*(5), 681–703. doi:10.1016/S0149-2063(03)00031-X

Leung, A. (2003). Different ties for different needs: Recruitment practices of entrepreneurial firms at different developmental phases. *Human Resource Management, 42*(4), 303–320. doi:10.1002/hrm.10092

Lin, W. -T. (2012). Family ownership and internationalization processes: Internationalization pace, internationalization scope, and internationalization rhythm. *European Management Journal, 30*(1), 47–56. doi:10.1016/j.emj.2011.10.003

Lobo, C. A., Fernandes, C. I. M. A. S., Ferreira, J. J. M., & Peris-Ortiz, M. (2020). Factors affecting SMEs' strategic decisions to approach international-markets. *European Journal of International Management, 14*(4), 617–639. doi:10.1504/EJIM.2020.107607

Lopez, L., Kundu, S., & Ciravegna, L. (2009). Born global or born regional? Evidence from an exploratory study in the Costa Rican software industry. *Journal of International Business Studies, 40*, 1228–1238. doi:10.1057/jibs.2008.69

Lu, J. W., & Beamish, P. W. (2001). The internationalization and performance of SMEs. *Strategic Management Journal, 22*(6/7), 565–586. http://www.jstor.org/stable/3094321

Luo, Y. (2000). Dynamic capabilities in international expansion. *Journal of World Business 35*(4), 355–378. doi:10.1016/S1090-9516(00)00043-2

Madison, K., Daspit, J. J., Turner, K., & Kellermanns, F. W. (2018). Family firm human resource practices: Investing the effects of professionalization and bifurcation bias on performance. *Journal of Business Research, 84*, 327–336. doi:10.1016/j.jbusres.2017.06.021

Madsen, T. K., & Servais, P. (1997). The internationalization of born globals: An evolutionary process? *International Business Review, 6*(6), 561–583. doi:10.1016/S0969-5931(97)00032-2

Majocchi, A., D'Angelo, A., Forlani, E., & Buck, T. (2018). Bifurcation bias and exporting: Can foreign work experience be an answer? Insight from European family SMEs. *Journal of World Business, 53*, 237–247. doi:10.1016/j.jwb.2017.11.005

Manolova, T., Manev, I. M., & Gyoshev, B. S. (2010). In good company: The role of personal and inter-firm networks for new-venture internationalization in a transition economy. *Journal of World Business, 45*(3), 257–265. doi:10.1016/j.jwb.2009.09.004

Marchington, M., & Grugulis, I. (2000). "Best Practice" human resource management: Perfect opportunity or dangerous illusion? *The International Journal of Human Resource Management, 11*, 1104–1124. doi:10.1080/095 85190050177184

Martineau, C., & Pastoriza, D. (2016). International involvement of established SMEs: A systematic review of antecedents, outcomes and moderators. *International Business Review, 25*, 458–470. doi:10.1016/j.ibusrev.2015.07.005

Mayrhofer W., Brewster C., & Farndale E. (2018). Future avenues for comparative human resource management. In C. Breswster, W. Mayrhofer, & E. Farndale (Eds.), *Handbook of research in comparative human resource management* (pp. 633–650). Cheltenham, UK: Edward Elgar Publishing.

McAuley, A. (1999). Entrepreneurial instant exporters in the Scottish arts and crafts sector. *Journal of International Marketing, 7*(4), 67–82. doi:10.1177/1069031X9900700405

Medcof, J. W., & Song, L. J. (2013). Exploration, exploitation and human resource management practices in cooperative and entrepreneurial HR configurations. *The International Journal of Human Resource Management, 24*(15), 2911–2926. doi:10.1080/09585192.2012.756055

Mejri, K., & Umemoto, K. (2010) Small- and medium-sized enterprise internationalization: Towards the knowledge-based model. *Journal of International Entrepreneurship, 8*, 156–167. doi:10.1007/s10843-010-0058-6

Melin, L. (1992). Internationalisation as a strategy process. *Strategic Management Journal, 13*, 99–118. doi:10.1002/smj.4250130908

Milliman, J., von Glinow, M. A., & Nathan, M. (1991). Organizational life cycles and strategic international human resource management in multinational companies: Implications for congruence theory. *The Academy of Management Review, 16*(2), 318–339. doi:10.2307/258864

Mohr, A., & Batsakis, G. (2017). Internationalization speed and firm performance: A study of the market-seeking expansion of retail MNEs. *Management International Review, 57*, 153–177. doi 10.1007/s11575-016-0284-9

Mohr, A. T., Fastoso, F., Wang, C., & Shirodkar, V. (2014). Testing the regional performance of multinational enterprises in the retail sector: The moderating effects of timing, speed and experience. *British Journal of Management, 25*(S1), 100–125. doi:10.1111/1467-8551.12013

Morley, M. J. (2007). Of infants and adolescents: Progress and pessimism in the development trajectory of international human resource management. Keynote Presentation to the 9th IHRM Conference, 12–15 June, Tallinn.

Morley, J. M., Slavic, A., Poór, J., & Berber, N. (2016). Training practices and organisational outcomes: A comparative analysis of domestic and internationally focused companies operating in the transition economies of Central & Eastern Europe. *Journal of East European Management Studies, 21*, 406–432.

Morley, M. J., Heraty, N., & Michailova, S. (Eds.) (2009). *Managing human resources in Central and Eastern Europe*. London and New York: Routledge.

Moš, O. (2017). An innovative approach to human resource management in small and medium enterprises: The SHARPEN project. *ACC Journal, 23*(2). doi:10.15240/tul/004/2017-2-006

Mudambi, R., & Zahra, S. (2007). The survival of international new ventures. *Journal of International Business Studies, 38,* 333–352. doi:10.1057/palgrave.jibs.8400264

Musteen, M., Datta, D. K., & Butts, M. M. (2014). Do international networks and foreign market knowledge facilitate SME internationalization? Evidence from the Czech Republic. *Entrepreneurship Theory and Practice, 38*(4), 749–774. doi:10.1111/etap.12025

Nummela, N., Puumalainen, K., & Saarenketo, S. (2005). International growth orientation of knowledge-intensive small firms. *Journal of International Entrepreneurship, 3*(1), 5–18. doi:10.1007/s10843-005-0350-z

Nummela, N., Saarenketo, S., & Puumalainen, K. (2004). Global mindset – A prerequisite for successful internationalization?. *Canadian Journal of Administrative Sciences, 21*(1), 51–64. doi:10.1111/j.1936-4490.2004.tb00322.x

Nummela, N., Vissak, T., & Francioni, B. (2022). The interplay of entrepreneurial and non-entrepreneurial internationalization: An illustrative case of an Italian SME. *International Entrepreneurship and Management Journal, 18,* 295–325. doi:10.1007/s11365-020-00673-y

O'Connor, C., & Joffe, H. (2020). Intercoder reliability in qualitative research: Debates and practical guidelines. *International Journal of Qualitative Methods, 19,* 1–13. doi:10.1177/1609406919899220

O'Donohue, W., & Torugsa, N. (2016). The moderating effect of 'green' HRM on the association between proactive environmental management and financial performance in small firms. *International Journal of Human Resource Management, 27*(2), 239–261.

OECD. (2015). *Taxation of SMEs in OECD and G20 countries.* OECD Tax Policy Studies No. 23. Paris: OECD Publishing. doi:10.17.87/9789264243507-3n

OECD. (2022). Trade by enterprise characteristics: Trade by size classes, ISIC Rev. 4. *OECD statistics on measuring globalisation (database).* doi:10.1787/data-00612-en (accessed 18 July 2022).

OECD. (n.d. a). *Making it easier for SMEs to trade in the global economy.* https://www.oecd.org/trade/topics/small-and-medium-enterprises-and-trade/ (accessed 18 July 2022).

OECD. (n.d. b). *Glossary for Barriers to SME Access to International Markets,* http://www.oecd.org/cfe/smes/glossaryforbarrierstosmeaccesstointernational markets.htm, (accessed 18 July 2022).

Office of the United States Trade Representatives. (n.d.). *Small and medium-sized enterprises – Advancing the interests of America's largest employers: Small and medium-sized businesses.* https://ustr.gov/trade-agreements/free-trade-agreements/trans-pacific-partnership/tpp-chapter-chapter-negotiating-8 (accessed 18 July 2022).

Onkelinx, J., Manolova, T. S., & Edelman, L. F. (2016). Human capital and SME internationalization: Empirical evidence from Belgium. *International Small Business Journal, 34*(6), 818–837. doi:10.1177/0266242615591856

Oviatt, B., & McDougall, P. P. (1994). Toward a theory of international new ventures. *Journal of International Business Studies, 25*(1), 45–64. doi:10.105 7/palgrave.jibs.8490193

Oviatt, B., & McDougall, P. P. (2005). Toward a theory of international new ventures. *Journal of International Business Studies, 36*, 29–41. doi:10.1057/ palgravejibs.8400128

Øyna, S., & Alon, I. (2018). A review of born globals. *International Studies of Management, & Organization, 48*(2), 157–180, doi:10.1080/00208825.2018. 1443737

Patel, P. C., Criaco, G., & Naldi, L. (2018). Geographic diversification and the survival of born-globals. *Journal of Management, 44*(5), 2008–2036. doi:10. 1177/0149206316635251

Paul, J., & Rosado-Serrano, A. (2019). Gradual internationalization vs Born Global/International new venture models: A review and research agenda. *International Marketing Review, 36*(6), 830–858. doi:10.1108/IMR-10-2018-0280

Paul, J., Parthasarathy, S., & Gupta., P. (2017). Exporting challenges of SMEs: A review and future research agenda. *Journal of World Business, 52*, 327–342. doi:10.1016/j.jwb.2017.01.003

Pauli, U. (2018). Talent management practices in polish small and medium enterprises. *Zarządzanie Zasobami Ludzkimi, 125*(6), 97–108.

Penrose, E. (1959). *The theory of the growth of the firm*. New York: John Wiley & Sons.

Perlmutter, H. V. (1969). The tortuous evolution of the multinational corporation. *Columbia Journal of World Business, 1*, 9–18.

Pezderka, N., & Sinkovics, R. R. (2011). A conceptualization of e-risk perceptions and implications for small firm active online internationalization. *International Business Review, 20*(4), 409–422. doi:10.1016/j.ibusrev.2010. 06.004

Piva, E., Rossi-Lamastra, C., & De Massis, A. (2013). Family firms and internationalization. An exploratory study on high-tech entrepreneurial ventures. *Journal of International Entrepreneurship, 11*, 108–129. doi:10.1007/ s10843-012-0100-y

Pla-Barber, J., & Escribá-Esteve, A. (2006). Accelerated internationalisation: Evidence from a late investor country. *International Marketing Review, 23*(3), 255–278. doi:10.1108/02651330610670442

Pocztowski, A., & Pauli, U. (2013). Profesjonalizacja zarządzania zasobami ludzkimi w małych i średnich przedsiębiorstwach. *Zarządzanie Zasobami Ludzkimi, 3–4*, 9–22.

Pocztowski, A., & Pauli, U. (2022). The impact of contextual factors on talent management practices in SMEs. *Human Systems Management, 41*, 87–101. doi:10.3233/HSM-211174

Pocztowski, A., Pauli, U., & Miś, A. (2021). *Talent management in small and medium enterprises. Context, practices and outcomes*. New York and London: Routledge.

Polish Agency for Enterprise Development. (2022). *Sukcesja w firmach rodzinnych, wsparcie MŚP w przekazywaniu biznesu.* https://www.parp.gov.pl/component/content/article/77802:sukcesja-w-firmach-rodzinnych-wsparcie-msp-w-przekazaniu-biznesu

Prange, C., & Verdier, S. (2011). Dynamic capabilities, internationalization processes and performance. *Journal of World Business, 46*(1), 126–133. doi:10.1016/j.jwb.2010.05.024

Prashantham, S., & Young, S. (2011). Post-entry speed of international new ventures. *Entrepreneurship Theory and Practice, 35*(2), 275–292. doi:10.1111/j.1540-6520.2009.00360.x

Psychogios, A., Szamosi, L. T., Prouska, R., & Brewster, C. (2016). A threefold framework for understanding HRM practices in South-Eastern European SMEs. *Employee Relations, 38*(3), 310–331. doi:10.1108/ER-07-2014-0078

Raby, S. O., & Gilman, M. W. (2012). Human resource management in small and medium-sized enterprises. In R. Kramar & J. Syed (Eds.), *Human resource management in a global context. A critical approach* (pp. 424–455). Basingstoke: Palgrave MacMillan.

Rastrollo-Horrillo, M. A., & Martin-Armario, J. (2019). Organisational barriers to nascent born-global growth: Learning from the inside. *Journal of International Entrepreneurship 17*(3), 454–473. doi:10.1007/s10843-019-00256-1

Rauch, A., & Hatak, I. (2016). A meta-analysis of different HR-enhancing practices and performance of small and medium sized firms. *Journal of Business Venturing, 31*(5), 485–504. doi:10.1016/j.jbusvent.2016.05.005

Reid, S. D. (1981). The decision-maker and export entry and expansion. *Journal of International Business Studies, 12*(2), 101–112. doi:10.1057/palgrave.jibs.8490581

Rennie, M. W. (1993). Global competitiveness: Born global. *McKinsey Quarterly, 4*, 45–52.

Rialp, A., Rialp, J., & Knight, G. A. (2005). The phenomenon of early internationalizing firms: What do we know after a decade (1993–2003) of scientific inquiry? *International Business Review, 14*, 147–166. doi:10.1016/j.ibusrev.2004.04.006

Rialp-Criado, A., Galván-Sánchez, I., & Suárez-Ortega, S. M. (2010). A configuration-holistic approach to born-global firms' strategy formations process. *European Management Journal, 28*(2). doi:108–12310.1016/j.emj.2009.05.001

Ripollé, M., Blesa, A., Hernández, M. A., & Isusi, I. (2018). More than job creation: Employee engagement in knowledge sharing and learning advantages of newness. In I. Mandl & V. Patrini (Eds.), *European Born Globals. Job creation in young international businesses* (pp. 128–147). London/New York: Routledge.

Romanello, R., & Chiarvesio, M. (2017). Turning point: When born globals enter post-entry stage. *International Journal of Entrepreneurship, 15*, 177–206. doi:10.1007/s10843-016-0192-x

Romanello, R., & Chiarvesio, M. (2019). Early internationalizing firms: 2004-2018. *Journal of International Entrepreneurship, 17,* 172–219. doi:10.1007/s10843-018-0241-8

Ruzzier, M., Antoncic, B., Hisrich, R. D., & Konečnik, M. (2007). Human capital and SME internationalization: a structural equation modeling study. *Canadian Journal of Administrative Sciences-revue Canadienne Des Sciences De L Administration, 24,* 15–29.

Ruzzier, M., Hisrich, R. D., & Antonic, B. (2006). SME internationalization research: Past, present, and future. *Journal of Small Business and Enterprise Development, 13*(4), 476–497. doi:10.1108/14626000610705705

Ruzzier, M., & Konecnik Ruzzier, M. (2015). On the relationship between firm size, resources, age at entry and internationalization: The case of Slovenian SMEs. *Journal of Business Economics and Management, 16*(1), 52–73. doi:10.3846/16111699.2012.745812

Sánchez-Marín, G., Meroño-Cerdán, Á. L., & Carrasco-Hernández, A. J. (2019). Formalized HR practices and firm performance: An empirical comparison of family and non-family firms. *The International Journal of Human Resource Management, 30*(7), 1084–1110. doi:10.1080/09585192.2017.1289547

Schwens, C., & Kabst, R. (2009). How early opposed to late internationalizers learn: Experience of others and paradigms of interpretation. *International Business Review, 18,* 509–522. doi:10.1016/j.ibusrev.2009.06.001

Sheehan, M. (2014). Human resource management and performance: Evidence from small and medium-sized firms. *International Small Business Journal, 32*(5), 545–570. doi:10.1177/0266242612465454

Shoham, A., Rose, G. M., & Albaum, G. S. (1995). Export motives, psychological distance and the EPRG framework. *Journal of Global Marketing, 8*(3–4), 9–37.

Sidor-Rządkowska, M. (2010). *Zarządzanie personelem w małej firmie.* Warszawa: Oficyna a Wolters Kluwer Business.

Simerly, R. L., & Li, M. (2000). Environmental dynamism, capital structure and performance: A theoretical integration and an empirical test. *Strategic Management Journal, 21*(1), 31–49. doi:10.1002/(SICI)1097-0266(200001)21:1<31::AID-SMJ76>3.0.CO;2-T

Sinkovics, N., Sinkovics, R. R., & "Bryan" Jean, R. (2013). The internet as an alternative path to internationalization? *International Marketing Review, 30*(2), 130–155. doi:10.1108/02651331311314556

Sleuwaegen, L., & Onkelinx, J. (2014). International commitment, post-entry growth and survival of international new ventures. *Journal of Business Venturing, 29*(1), 106–120. doi:10.1016/j.jbusvent.2013.01.001.

Steinhäuser, V. P. S., Paula, F. D., & de Macedo-Soares, T. D. L. V. (2021). Internationalization of SMEs: A systematic review of 20 years of research. *Journal of International Entrepreneurship, 19,* 164–195. doi:10.1007/s10843-020-00271-7

Storey, D. J. (1994). *Understanding the small business sector*. London: Routledge.

Stöttinger, B., & Schlegelmilch, B. B. (1998). Explaining export development through psychic distance: Enlightening or elusive? *International Marketing Review, 15*(5), 357–372. doi:10.1108/02651339810236353

Strużyna, J. (2002). *Doskonalenie jakości zarządzania zasobami ludzkimi w małych firmach.* Katowice, Wydawnictwo Akademii Ekonomicznej.

Surdu, I., Greve, H. R., & Benito, G. R. G. (2021). Back to basics: Behavioral theory and internationalization. *Journal of International Business Studies, 52*, 1047–1068. doi:10.1057/s41267-020-00388-w

Tan, A., Brewer, P., & Liesch, P. W. (2007). Before the first export decision: Internationalisation readiness in the pre-export phase. *International Business Review, 16*(3), 294–309.

Tarique, I., Briscoe, D., & Schuler, R. (2016). *International human resource management. Policies and practices for multinational enterprises* (5th ed.). New York and London: Routledge.

Tuomisalo, T., & Leppaaho, T. (2019). Learning in international new ventures: A systematic review. *International Business Review, 28*, 463–481. doi:10.1016/j.ibusrev.2018.11.005

Turcan, R. V., & Juho, A. (2014). What happens to international new venture beyond start-up: An exploratory study. *Journal of International Entrepreneurship, 12*, 129–145. doi:10.1007/s10843-014-0124-6

Vermeulen, F., & Barkema, H. (2002). Pace, rhythm, and scope: Process dependence in building a profitable multinational corporation. *Strategic Management Journal, 23*(7), 637–653. doi:10.1002/smj.243

Vissak, T., Francioni, B., & Freeman, S. (2020). Foreign market entries, exits and re-entries: The role of knowledge, network relationships and decision-making logic. *International Business Review, 29*(1), 101592. doi:10.1016/j.ibusrev.2019.101592

Vuorio, A., Torkkeli, L., & Sainio, L.-M. (2020). Service innovation and internationalization in SMEs: Antecedences and profitability outcomes. *Journal of International Entrepreneurship, 18*, 92–123. doi:10.1007/s10843-019-00266-z

Wapshott, R., & Mallett, O. (2016). *Managing human resources in small and medium-sized enterprises.* New York, NY: Routledge.

Weerawardena, J., Mort, G. S., Liesch, P. W., & Knight, G. (2007). Conceptualizing accelerated internationalization in the born global firm: A dynamic capabilities perspective. *Journal of World Business, 42*(3), 294–306. doi:10.1016/j.jwb.2007.04.004

Welch, L. S., & Luostarinen, R. K. (1988). Internationalization: Evolution of a concept. *Journal of General Management, 14*(2), 34–55. doi:10.1177/03063 0708801400203

Welch, L. S., & Luostarinen, R. K. (1993). Inward-outward connections in internationalization. *Journal of International Marketing, 1*(3), 44–56. doi:10.1177/1069031X9300100104

Wernerfelt, B. (1984). A resource-based view of the firm. *Strategic Management Journal, 5*, 171–180. doi:10.1002/smj.4250050207

WTO. (2016). *World trade report 2016 – Levelling the trading field for SMEs,* https://www.wto.org/english/res_e/booksp_e/world_trade_report16_e.pdf (accessed 09 September 2022).

Xing, Y., Liu, Y., Boojihawon (Roshan), D. K., & Tarba, S.(2020). Entrepreneurial team and strategic agility: A conceptual framework and research agenda. *Human Resource Management Review, 30*, 100696. doi:10.1016/j.hrmr.2019.100696

Yin, R. K. (2013). *Case study research. Design and methods* (5th ed.). London, UK: Sage Publications.

Young, S., Hamill, J., Wheeler, C., & Davies, J. R. (1989). *International market entry and development: Strategies and management.* Hemel Hempstead: Harvester Wheatsheaf.

Zaheer, S. (1995). Overcoming the liability of foreignness. *Academy of Management Journal, 38*(2), 341–363. doi:10.5465/256683

Zaheer, S., & Mosakowski, E. (1997). The dynamics of the liability of foreignness: A global study of survival in financial services. *Strategic Management Journal, 18*(6), 439–463.

Zahra, S. A. (2005). A theory of international new ventures: A decade of research. *Journal of International Business Studies, 36*(1), 20–28. doi:10.1057/palgrave.jibs.8400118

Zhou, L. (2007). The effects of entrepreneurial proclivity and foreign market knowledge on early internationalization. *Journal of World Business, 42*, 281–293. doi:10.1016/j.jwb.2007.04.009

Zhou, L., & Wu, A. (2014). Earliness of internationalization and performance outcomes: Exploring the moderating effects of venture age and international commitment. *Journal of World Business, 49*, 132–142. doi:10.1016/j.jwb.2013.10.001

Zhou, Y., Hong, Y., & Liu, J. (2013). Internal commitment or external collaboration? The impact of human resource management systems on firm innovation and performance. *Human Resource Management, 52*(2), 263–288. doi:10.1002/hrm.21527

Zucchella, A., Danicolai, S., & Palamara, G. (2007). The drivers of the early internationalization of the firm. *Journal of World Business, 42*(3), 268–280. doi:10.1016/j.jwb.2007.04.008

Index